Project Management & Entrepreneurship

Dr. Santosh Kumar Pandey
Ph.D., MPhil, MBA, UGC NET and MSc,
Associate professor,
PSIT College of Higher Education Kanpur (UP), India

Prof. (Dr.) Bhagwan Jagwani
Director,
PSIT College of Higher Education Kanpur (UP), India

NOTION PRESS

Dedicated to my father

Late Shri Ram Narayan Pandey

Table of Contents

Preface

The importance of Project Management & Entrepreneurship is well-known in the Management field. The overwhelming response to our book on Operation Research inspired me to write this book. The book is structured to cover the key aspects of the subject of Project Management & Entrepreneurship.

The book uses plain and lucid language to explain the fundamentals of this subject. The book provides a logical method of explaining various complicated concepts and stepwise methods to explain important topics. Each chapter is well supported with necessary illustrations, practical examples, and solved problems. All the chapters in the book are arranged in it proper sequence that permits each topic to build upon earlier studies. All care has been taken to make students comfortable in understanding the basic concepts of the subject.

The book not only covers the entire scope of the subject but also explains the philosophy of the subject. This makes the understanding of this subject clearer and makes it more interesting. The book will be very useful not only to the students but also to the subject teachers. The students have to omit nothing and possibly have to cover nothing more.

– Dr. Santosh Kumar Pandey

About Authors

Dr. Santosh Kumar Pandey is working as an Associate professor, at PSIT College of Higher Education Kanpur (UP), India. With more than 14 years of teaching experience. He has worked at Axis Institute of Planning and Management for the last 10 years with various responsibilities like Chief Proctor, Head of Admission and Marketing along with his teaching and other academic activities. He has authored 2 books, 14 international and 10 national peer-reviewed technical publications. He also attended more than 10 AICTE-approved conferences held in various engineering colleges and universities. He has done his research on the sale-related issues of the automotive industry. He has been awarded "Best Teacher" by Alliance Clubs International and also by IIMA, Kanpur.

Dr. Bhagwan Jagwani is a Management Professor, Trainer, and Consultant in Finance & Accounting. He is presently the Director of PSIT College of Higher Education, Kanpur. His previous associations include Group Director at Allenhouse Group of Institutions, Kanpur; Campus Head at ICFAI Academy, Hyderabad; and Professor and Finance Area Head at Dr. Gaur Hari Singhania Institute of Management & Research, Kanpur.

Possessing a work experience of 25+ years in industry and academia, Prof. Bhagwan is professionally qualified as a Company Secretary and is presently a 'Fellow Member' of the Institute of Company Secretaries of India. He also holds a PhD and a Post Graduate degree in Commerce. Besides this, he is UGC-NET qualified and possesses various certifications in 'Business Analytics', 'International Finance', and 'Financial Derivatives from renowned institutions. He is also a certified trainer of Predictive and Descriptive Analytics.

To date, Dr. Bhagwan has conducted over 50 Management and Faculty Development programs and training sessions in India and abroad and has presented and published research papers in national and international conferences, ABDC & Scopus-indexed and foreign journals. His research paper based on his doctoral thesis was awarded

2nd prize in a 'Doctoral Student' Paper Competition organized by AIMS International, Houston, USA.

Dr. Bhagwan has also been a recipient of 'Best Paper Presenter' and 'Best Faculty Guide' awards. Born in the Philippines (Southeast Asia), Dr. Bhagwan strongly believes in the law of 'Karma', and for him, 'Success is how high you bounce, after hitting the bottom'.

Acknowledgments

Words fall short of thanking the Almighty God who has given us this life, family, opportunities, and education. Therefore, it is indeed a matter of great pleasure to express the deepest gratitude for a never-ending shower of His blessings and to thank all those who gave a helping hand in the completion of this work.

First and foremost, I would like to express our appreciation and sincere gratitude to my research supervisors. I have been amazingly fortunate to have the best mentor and advisor I could have ever wished for. I learned a lot from his advice and useful insights throughout our research. Their regular encouragement regarding referred publications helped me a lot to overcome my doubts and finish this work.

We are thankful to all our friends working in various universities and colleges, and our deepest gratitude to my parents, my wife, siblings, and all other family members for their loving support and for always standing behind me to cheer me in good times and encourage me in bad times.

We would also like to express my sincere thanks to the members of management, colleagues, teaching staff, and non-teaching staff of our colleges for assisting me throughout my writing work.

– Dr. Santosh Kumar Pandey

Unit – 1

Entrepreneurship

Entrepreneurship: need, scope, Entrepreneurial competencies & traits, Factors affecting entrepreneurial development, Entrepreneurial motivation (Mc Clellend's Achievement motivation theory), conceptual model of entrepreneurship, entrepreneur vs. entrepreneur; Classification of entrepreneurs; Entrepreneurial Development Programmes

---

1.1 Defining Entrepreneur

An entrepreneur is an individual who initiates, develops, organizes, and manages a business venture to make a profit. Being an entrepreneur requires creativity, drive, and risk-taking. An entrepreneur must be able to identify opportunities in the market, create strategies to capitalize on them, and then execute those strategies with determination.

Successful entrepreneurs are often able to think outside of the box and make decisions quickly to stay ahead of their competitors. They can create something new that will benefit society as well as themselves.

1.1.1 A vision of an entrepreneur

An entrepreneur should have a vision focused on creating value for customers and society. They should strive to work on innovative products and services to make the world better. They should also focus on building strong relationships with customers, partners, investors, and employees.

It will help them build trust and loyalty in the long run. Entrepreneurs must also have the courage to take risks and be willing to learn from their mistakes. Lastly, they must be focused on their goals while being flexible enough to adapt to changing market conditions.

Skills every entrepreneur needs to succeed

1. ***Finance skills:*** Every entrepreneur requires a good understanding of finance to succeed in business. It includes managing cash flow, budgeting, forecasting, and understanding the various financial instruments available. Having sound financial knowledge helps entrepreneurs make informed decisions that will help them achieve their goals. It also helps them identify potential risks and opportunities that may arise in the future. Understanding and managing finances is an essential skill for entrepreneurs looking to succeed in the long run.

2. ***Communication skills:*** Communication skills are essential for entrepreneurs to be successful. Entrepreneurs must communicate effectively with customers, partners, employees, and other stakeholders. Good communication skills can help entrepreneurs build relationships, create trust, and increase their chances of success. Additionally, entrepreneurs must be able to articulate their ideas clearly and concisely to attract potential investors and customers. Having good communication skills can also help entrepreneurs better manage their teams in resolving conflicts quickly.

3. ***Leadership skills:*** In today's competitive business world, having the right leadership skills is essential for entrepreneurs to succeed. Leadership skills are not just about managing but also about inspiring and motivating them to reach their goals. It involves

- Ability to make decisions

- Set goals

- Inspire others and build a team that works together toward success.

As an entrepreneur, it is important to develop your leadership skills to achieve success in your venture.

1.1.2 Characteristics of an Entrepreneur

The entrepreneurial mindset combines several different skills that require careful development for the achievement of a business idea. For example, an entrepreneur must be able to balance an understanding of how business works — including from a financial and operational perspective — with a drive for innovation. Entrepreneurship means understanding when you have an opening in the marketplace that no other provider is meeting and having the business sense to know how to go after this new opportunity at the right time.

A successful entrepreneur will possess many abilities and characteristics, including the ability to be:

Entrepreneurial drive stems from qualities like these, just as an entrepreneur's ability to succeed will depend on developing these abilities.

1.2 Defining Entrepreneurship

Entrepreneurship is the process of identifying, creating, and pursuing opportunities to develop new products, services, or business ventures. It involves the willingness to take risks, the ability to innovate, and the capacity to mobilize resources effectively to bring ideas to life and create value in the market.

Entrepreneurship is a broad and evolving concept, and various scholars, practitioners, and organizations have provided different definitions based on their perspectives. Below are some of the most prominent definitions of **entrepreneurship**:

1. Joseph Schumpeter's Definition

Joseph Schumpeter, a renowned economist, is often considered one of the founders of modern entrepreneurship theory. He defined **entrepreneurship** as:

"The process of creative destruction."

Schumpeter believed entrepreneurs are individuals who introduce innovations, create new products, and bring about economic changes by disrupting existing market structures. They are not merely risk-takers but agents of change who replace outdated business models with new ones.

2. Peter Drucker's Definition

Peter Drucker, a management expert, defined **entrepreneurship** as:

"The act of innovation that endows resources with a new capacity to create wealth."

Drucker emphasized that entrepreneurship is about innovation—identifying opportunities, creating value, and solving problems by deploying resources in a new or different way.

3. Howard Stevenson's Definition

Howard Stevenson, a professor at Harvard Business School, provided a widely-accepted definition of **entrepreneurship**:

"The pursuit of opportunity without regard to resources currently controlled."

Stevenson focused on the idea that entrepreneurship involves seizing opportunities and pursuing new ventures even if the entrepreneur doesn't initially have all the necessary resources. It highlights the importance of vision and determination in the entrepreneurial journey.

4. The Global Entrepreneurship Monitor (GEM) Definition

The **Global Entrepreneurship Monitor (GEM)**, an international research project on entrepreneurship, defines **entrepreneurship** as:

"The process of identifying, developing, and bringing a vision to life by creating a new venture or business."

This definition emphasizes the entire process involved in turning an idea or vision into a reality by creating a business, focusing on both the opportunity-seeking aspect and the development of a new entity.

5. Drucker and His Concept of Innovation

In a similar vein, Peter Drucker also defined **entrepreneurship** in terms of the ability to see and exploit opportunities for **innovation**. He noted:

"Entrepreneurship is not just starting a new business but creating and developing something new."

This underscores the idea that entrepreneurship is about finding or creating something new (whether it be products, services, processes, or business models) that addresses a need or creates value in society.

6. Richard Cantillon's Definition

Richard Cantillon, an early economist, defined **entrepreneurship** as:

"The person who pays a certain price for a good or service and resells it at an uncertain price, thereby taking on the risk of the enterprise."

Cantillon emphasized the concept of risk-taking and uncertainty in entrepreneurship. The entrepreneur's role is to manage risk by acquiring and reselling goods or services, where the future price is uncertain.

7. Steve Jobs' Definition

Steve Jobs, the co-founder of Apple, approached **entrepreneurship** from a more visionary angle:

"The people who are crazy enough to think they can change the world are the ones who do."

Jobs' definition focuses on entrepreneurs being individuals who dare to dream big, challenge the status quo, and create transformative products or services that reshape the world.

8. The Oxford Dictionary Definition

The **Oxford English Dictionary** defines **entrepreneurship** as:

"The activity of setting up a business or businesses, taking on financial risks in the hope of profit."

This definition highlights the fundamental economic aspect of entrepreneurship—starting and managing a business while bearing the risk of financial loss in the hopes of generating a profit.

9. Schumpeter's Innovation Definition

Schumpeter's concept of **entrepreneurship** revolves around **innovation**:

"Entrepreneurship is the doing of new things or the doing of things that are already being done in a new way."

This definition focuses on the act of **innovation** as a key component of entrepreneurship, asserting that true entrepreneurs drive economic development through new ideas, new technologies, or new methods of doing things.

10. Entrepreneurship as a Process (By David H. Holt)

David H. Holt defined **entrepreneurship** as:

"The process of discovering, evaluating, and exploiting opportunities."

This definition emphasizes the systematic process that entrepreneurs go through—identifying and seizing opportunities, assessing their feasibility, and then exploiting them to create value and drive business success.

11. The UNCTAD Definition (United Nations Conference on Trade and Development)

The **United Nations Conference on Trade and Development (UNCTAD)** defines **entrepreneurship** as:

"The creation and development of new businesses, typically involving the assumption of financial risks in the hope of profit, by individuals or groups."

This definition ties entrepreneurship to the **economic development** of nations and communities, recognizing it as a key driver of innovation and economic growth.

12. The Small Business Administration (SBA) Definition (USA)

The **U.S. Small Business Administration** (SBA) defines **entrepreneurship** as:

"The process of starting and operating your own business to make a profit."

It defines entrepreneurship in terms of both the personal initiative (starting the business) and the goal of making a profit.

1.2.1 Key Aspects of Entrepreneurship

Key aspects of entrepreneurship include:

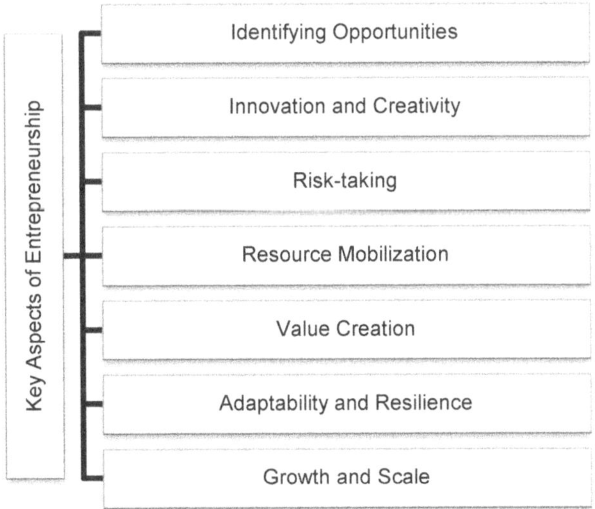

- ***Identifying Opportunities:*** Entrepreneurs have a keen eye for recognizing opportunities in the market. They identify unmet needs, gaps, or problems that can be solved through innovative solutions.

- ***Innovation and Creativity:*** Entrepreneurship is inherently creative and innovative. Entrepreneurs develop new ideas, products, or services that differentiate them from existing offerings in the market.

- ***Risk-taking:*** Entrepreneurship involves taking calculated risks. Entrepreneurs understand that there is uncertainty and potential failure associated with their ventures, but they are willing to take risks in pursuit of their goals

- ***Resource Mobilization:*** Entrepreneurs need to mobilize resources, including financial capital, human capital, and physical assets, to turn their ideas into reality. This may involve securing funding, building teams, and establishing partnerships or networks.

- ***Value Creation:*** The ultimate goal of entrepreneurship is to create value. This can take various forms, such as economic value through profitable business ventures, social value through addressing societal needs, or environmental value through sustainable practices.

- ***Adaptability and Resilience:*** Entrepreneurship often involves navigating challenges and setbacks. Entrepreneurs need to be adaptable and resilient, willing to pivot their strategies or adjust their approaches in response to changing market conditions or unexpected obstacles.

- ***Growth and Scale:*** While not all entrepreneurial ventures aim for rapid growth or scale, many entrepreneurs aspire to grow their businesses over time. This may involve expanding into new markets, increasing market share, or scaling operations to reach a larger customer base.

Entrepreneurship plays a crucial role in driving economic development, innovation, and job creation. It empowers individuals to pursue their passions, build businesses that align with their values, and contribute to the growth and dynamism of the economy.

1.2.2 Different Types of Entrepreneurship

Although profit is the chief motivator in entrepreneurship, it sometimes focuses on other aspects such as solving a problem or creating an impact. Let's see how the role of entrepreneurship changes with these different motivations.

- ***Social Entrepreneurship:*** Socially conscious businesses are focused on solving problems related to education, food, and economic inequality. The primary goal of such businesses is to raise funds for society's benefit and work towards development in specific areas such as health, community development, and poverty alleviation. They are sometimes referred to as non-profit organizations.

- ***Innovation Entrepreneurship:*** This type of entrepreneurship involves new inventions and ideas. Firms aim to deliver unique products or services that other businesses haven't covered. Innovation entrepreneurship often relies on technology and needs significant investment to get off the ground.

- ***Big Business Entrepreneurship:*** Big businesses have defined life cycles. They grow and thrive in the market by providing new and innovative products that relate to their main product. They try to expand their customer base, gain new market shares, and attempt to meet changing industry demands. Several businesses have been known to purchase smaller organizations and delegate innovation.

- ***Small Business Entrepreneurship:*** Local restaurants, pop-up stores, and dry cleaners are a few examples of small business entrepreneurship. Such businesses rely on providing new and enhanced versions of their existing products and services. Profits are primarily used for sustaining instead of scaling and expansion.

- ***Scalable Start-Up Business Entrepreneurship:*** This type of entrepreneurship is rooted in a vision and mission of changing the world. Start-up entrepreneurs attract investors who will believe in their dreams, support them, and help them think outside the box. The model is both experimental and scalable, which is why it's crucial to hire the right people to support the founder's dream. They're answerable to stakeholders who want a return on the capital invested.

1.3 Need for Entrepreneurship

Entrepreneurship isn't easy; in fact, a majority of businesses fail but that shouldn't stop you from pursuing your dream. It's an instrument of social change and has proven to provide continuous opportunities for growth. It plays a vital role in the economy and encourages people to bring new and innovative ideas to market. Here are several factors that highlight the need for entrepreneurship in today's fast-paced world.

- ***Encourages innovation:*** A majority of entrepreneurs solve challenges in society through technological innovations. For example, TartanSense — a Bangalore-based start-up provides an AI-based Robot vehicle to be used in farms for weed management. It reduces chemical usage and helps farmers avoid unnecessary costs.

- ***Creates jobs:*** Entrepreneurship generates employment. Once a new business gets launched, it requires people who can drive that mission and vision forward. Entrepreneurs take the risk of employing even themselves. As the business continues to grow, the need to hire more people also increases. Take any leading education technology start-up for example. Some of them have become unicorns and opened branches across the globe.

- ***Improves standard of living:*** Entrepreneurship increases income levels, therefore improving standards of living. Entrepreneurs identify challenges in the lives of customers and provide appropriate business solutions. Additionally, they hire new employees who receive remuneration and this income gets circulated in the economy. All of the spending and salaries generate incremental wealth, therefore improving standards of living.

- ***Introduces visible change:*** You need to dream big and take risks if you want to be a successful entrepreneur. As you progress to solving existing challenges and gaps in society, you take responsibility for impacting various sections of society. A majority of businesses strive to make the world a better place by contributing to socio-economic development through their products and services.

- ***Contributes to research and development:*** New products and services need to be tested before they can be launched. In the process, entrepreneurs are encouraged to invest their resources into effective research and development. Even after businesses get funding, entrepreneurs continue to prioritize research and development by creating educational institutes. This further encourages the next generation of entrepreneurs to take risks and pursue their dreams.

1.4 Scope of Entrepreneurship

The scope of entrepreneurship is vast and encompasses a wide range of opportunities and activities. Here are some key dimensions of the scope of entrepreneurship:

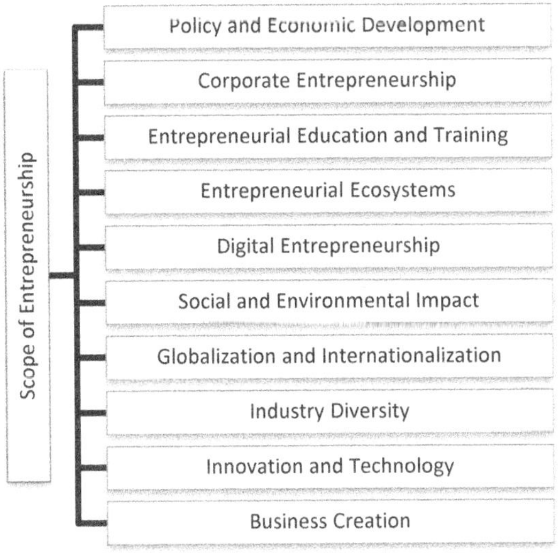

- ***Business Creation:*** At its core, entrepreneurship involves the creation of new businesses or ventures. This includes start-ups, small and medium-sized enterprises (SMEs), as well as larger corporations launched by entrepreneurs.

- ***Innovation and Technology:*** Entrepreneurship drives innovation and technological advancement across various industries and sectors. Entrepreneurs develop new products, services, processes, and business models that disrupt existing markets, create new industries, and address emerging needs and opportunities.

- ***Industry Diversity:*** Entrepreneurship spans diverse industries and sectors, including technology, healthcare, finance, retail, manufacturing, agriculture, education, and social services.

Entrepreneurs identify opportunities for business creation and innovation in virtually every sector of the economy.

- ***Globalization and Internationalization:*** Entrepreneurship is increasingly global, with entrepreneurs seeking opportunities beyond national borders. Globalization enables entrepreneurs to access international markets, talent, capital, and resources, facilitating cross-border collaboration and expansion.

- ***Social and Environmental Impact:*** Social entrepreneurship addresses social, environmental, and humanitarian challenges through innovative business solutions. Entrepreneurs develop enterprises that create positive social and environmental impacts, such as providing clean energy, improving healthcare access, addressing poverty, and promoting sustainability.

- ***Digital Entrepreneurship:*** The digital economy has opened up new avenues for entrepreneurship, with opportunities in e-commerce, digital platforms, software development, online services, and digital marketing. Digital entrepreneurship leverages technology to create scalable and disruptive businesses with global reach.

- ***Entrepreneurial Ecosystems:*** Entrepreneurship is supported by vibrant entrepreneurial ecosystems comprising various stakeholders, including government agencies, educational institutions, investors, mentors, incubators, accelerators, and networking organizations. These ecosystems provide infrastructure, funding, mentorship, and support services to nurture and sustain entrepreneurial ventures.

- ***Entrepreneurial Education and Training:*** Entrepreneurship education and training programs equip aspiring entrepreneurs with the knowledge, skills, and mindset needed to start and grow successful businesses. Educational institutions offer courses, workshops, and experiential learning opportunities in entrepreneurship, fostering a culture of innovation and risk-taking.

- ***Corporate Entrepreneurship:*** Entrepreneurship or corporate entrepreneurship involves entrepreneurial activities within established organizations. Corporate entrepreneurs identify and pursue opportunities for innovation, growth, and transformation within the company, driving entrepreneurial initiatives such as new product development, process improvements, and corporate venturing.

- ***Policy and Economic Development:*** Governments play a crucial role in fostering an enabling environment for entrepreneurship through supportive policies, regulations, incentives, and infrastructure investments. Entrepreneurship policies aim to promote business creation, innovation, job growth, and economic development, contributing to overall prosperity and competitiveness.

1.5 Factors of Entrepreneurial Development

Several factors can influence the development of entrepreneurship within a society or economy. These factors can vary depending on the context, but some of the most significant ones include:

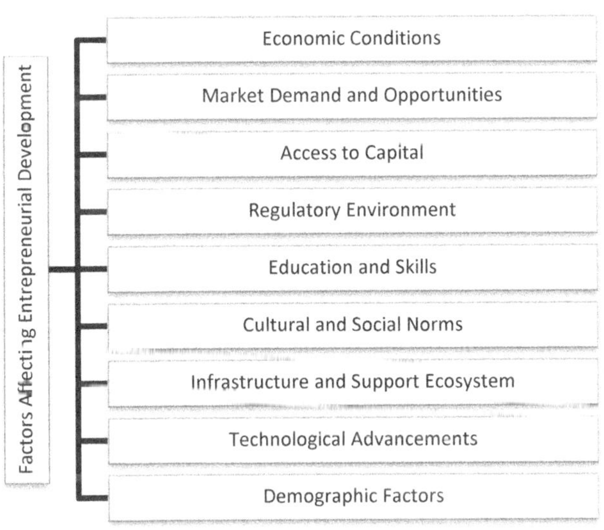

- ***Economic Conditions:*** Economic factors such as GDP growth, inflation rate, interest rates, and availability of credit can significantly impact entrepreneurship. A stable economy with favorable conditions for business growth and investment tends to encourage entrepreneurial activity.

- ***Market Demand and Opportunities:*** Entrepreneurship often thrives in environments with high demand for new products or services and abundant market opportunities. Emerging industries, technological advancements, and changing consumer preferences can create fertile ground for entrepreneurial ventures.

- ***Access to Capital:*** Access to financing is critical for aspiring entrepreneurs to start and grow their businesses. Factors such as the availability of venture capital, angel investment networks, government grants, and ease of accessing loans from financial institutions can influence entrepreneurial development.

- ***Regulatory Environment:*** Government policies and regulations play a significant role in shaping the entrepreneurial landscape. Entrepreneur-friendly policies, such as simplified business registration procedures, tax incentives for small businesses, and supportive regulatory frameworks, can encourage entrepreneurial activity.

- ***Education and Skills:*** Education and skills development are vital for nurturing an entrepreneurial mindset and equipping individuals with the knowledge and capabilities to start and manage businesses successfully. Entrepreneurship education programs, vocational training, and access to mentorship and networking opportunities can foster an entrepreneurial culture.

- ***Cultural and Social Norms:*** Cultural attitudes towards risk-taking, failure, and success can significantly influence entrepreneurial behavior. Cultures that celebrate innovation, reward entrepreneurship and embrace failure as a learning opportunity tend to have higher rates of entrepreneurial activity.

- ***Infrastructure and Support Ecosystem:*** Access to supportive infrastructure and resources, such as co-working spaces, incubators, accelerators, and business support services, can facilitate the development and growth of entrepreneurial ventures. Strong support ecosystems provide entrepreneurs with access to networks, mentors, and expertise, helping them navigate challenges and accelerate their growth.

- ***Technological Advancements:*** Technological innovations can both create new opportunities for entrepreneurship and disrupt traditional industries, leading to the emergence of new business models and entrepreneurial ventures. Access to technology and digital infrastructure can lower barriers to entry for aspiring entrepreneurs and enable innovative solutions to societal challenges.

- ***Demographic Factors:*** Demographic trends, such as population growth, age distribution, urbanization, and workforce composition, can influence entrepreneurial dynamics. For example, young populations with high levels of education and urbanization tend to have a higher propensity for entrepreneurship.

Overall, a combination of these factors shapes the entrepreneurial environment within a society or economy, influencing the prevalence, nature, and success of entrepreneurial ventures. Governments, policymakers, educational institutions, and other stakeholders play important roles in creating an ecosystem that fosters entrepreneurial development and unlocks its potential for economic growth and innovation.

1.6 Entrepreneurial Competencies & Traits

Entrepreneurial Competencies & Traits refer to the set of skills, knowledge, and personal characteristics that enable individuals to identify opportunities, take calculated risks, and successfully navigate the challenges of starting and running a business. These competencies and traits are crucial for entrepreneurs as they shape their ability to innovate, solve problems, and adapt to dynamic business environments. Understanding and cultivating these qualities can significantly enhance an entrepreneur's potential for success, empowering them to effectively manage their ventures and drive growth.

1.6.1 Introduction Entrepreneurial Competencies

Due to globalization, liberalization, and privatization, entrepreneurs are facing many challenges and hurdles for the survival of the enterprise in the globalized era. Many entrepreneurs have started their enterprises due to the lucrative benefits of entrepreneurship. However, only a few run their business successfully while many others suffer huge losses due to various problems. Now questions arise, why few entrepreneurs are successful and others not? Is there any difference between the successful and unsuccessful entrepreneurs? The obvious answer is yes. The success of a business depends on the attitude of entrepreneurs and the qualities she or he possesses. The skills, knowledge, and other personal traits that an entrepreneur possesses are called entrepreneurial competencies. Due to these competencies, entrepreneurs can perform their business tasks better than others. To run any entrepreneurial activity successfully, competencies are very essential. For modern-era entrepreneurs, it is very important to have an understanding of entrepreneurial competencies. Along with understanding, it is also very crucial to identify the in-born competencies and required competencies to develop the full range of entrepreneurial competencies. Now, the next question arises, whether these competencies can be injected or developed? There are various arguments for this question. Let us try to understand in detail the term competence and competencies and other related issues in this module.

1.6.1.1 Meaning or Concept of Competency

To understand the meaning or concept of competency, it is important to know the term 'Competence' because the term competency originated from the word competence. Understanding of competence concept will help to develop a clear idea about competency.

Various academicians defined these terms differently.

Boyatzis describes competence as the characteristics of an entrepreneur that result in the form of superior or effective performance in the business activity.

Based on this definition, we can describe that competence is the underlying characteristic of an entrepreneur through which she/he performs well. These underlying characteristics include personal traits such as knowledge, skills, personality, attitude, etc.

Hogg has defined competency as the demonstration of characteristics including skills and abilities, which result in superior business performance.

United Nations Industrial Development Corporation (UNIDO) has defined competency as skills, knowledge, and other attributes that help an entrepreneur perform tasks effectively and efficiently.

We can say entrepreneurial competence is the mix of skills, knowledge, and behavioral attributes of an entrepreneur that affect the performance of one's. Due to these attributes, few entrepreneurs perform well while others lack. Competency helps an entrepreneur in the effective and efficient functioning of an enterprise. Competency is the application of skill set, knowledge, and attitude for better performance on the job. It is the major differentiator between successful and unsuccessful entrepreneurs.

In practice, competency means, how an entrepreneur is using his acquired knowledge and skills. For example, if an entrepreneur is having B.Tech. (Computer Science) degree, and he is using his knowledge and skills in the automation of the enterprises, it is his competency.

Generally, the attributes of competency are not known to individual concern and that is the reason behind the poor performance of the business.

1.6.1.2 Competence versus Competency

Most of the time, people use competence and competency interchangeably, which means both are the same. Now, the question arises, if both are the same then why there is a need to discuss both terms separately?

Famous academicians McClelland describes that both the terms i.e. competence and competency are not the same and have different meanings.

The basic difference between the two is that competence is the underlying characteristic of an entrepreneur and competency is the behavioural aspect of the characteristics. The difference between both can be understood with the help of the following points:

1. Competence is skill-based while competency is behavior-based

2. Competence covers the standard attained in one's life whereas competency is the manner of behaviour.

3. Competence means what is measured and competency means how the standard is achieved.

Based on the above points, we can describe that competence means what people can do while competency means how people do it. We can also describe competence as skills and the performance standard achieved, while competency refers to the behavioral aspect through which the performance standard is achieved.

1.6.1.3 Attributes of Entrepreneurial Competency

In the above section, we have discussed the difference between competence and competency, and also understand that both are complementary to each other. In this section, you will learn about the main elements or attributes of entrepreneurial competency. The following are the three major attributes or components of entrepreneurial competency:

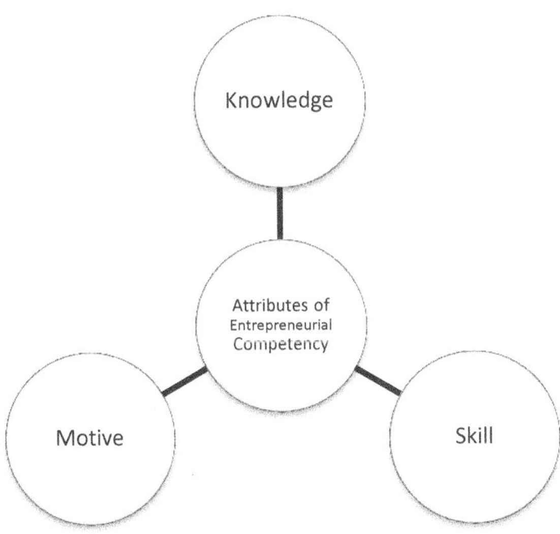

Let us try to understand these three attributes of entrepreneurial competency in detail with the help of examples.

Knowledge: Knowledge means gathering information and retention of gathered information for further application to complete tasks. Knowledge is very important to complete any task but not sufficient. For example, an individual can understand the process of setting up an enterprise by reading various books and further, she/he can describe the various aspects of business. But, mere reading and description will not enable the individual to establish the enterprise. We see in the real world that many entrepreneurs have full knowledge of business but fail miserably during the actual performance of the business tasks. This failure of entrepreneurs suggests that entrepreneurs also require something else to perform the task well. And this something extra is skills to use or translate the knowledge into application.

Skill: Skill simply means demonstration ability of knowledge which results in something that can be observed or seen. In other words, we can say it is a sequence of behaviors through which an entrepreneur applies his knowledge and creates a system that can be observed by others. For example, when an entrepreneur applies his gathered information to create and run a successful enterprise, it is her/his skill.

Knowledge can be acquired by reading and gathering information while skill is acquired by practice. This implies that both knowledge and skill are important to run an enterprise successfully.

Motive: The third important element of competence is motive. We can define motive as one's attitude and behavior to achieve the goal. Famous behavioral scientist McClelland termed motive as 'Achievement Motivation'. An entrepreneur can achieve success in his venture only if he has the motivation to achieve success. The continuous motive of success and achievement directs an entrepreneur to perform the job successfully. If we continue the above example, we can say, that an entrepreneur can achieve success only if he has the motivation to set and run an enterprise.

1.6.1.4 Features of Entrepreneurial Competencies

After discussing attributes of entrepreneurial competencies, we can enlist the features of competencies which are as follows:

- Entrepreneurial competencies are the underlying characteristics of an entrepreneur.

- It leads to the demonstration of knowledge that can be observed.

- Competencies must lead to superior performance.

- Entrepreneurial competencies can be acquired through information and practice.

1.6.1.5 Model of Competency

Khanka (2012) suggests a model of entrepreneurial competency through mathematical equation by using the above-discussed attributes of entrepreneurial competency.

Competency = Competence + Commitment

Where:

Competence = Knowledge * Skills

Commitment = One's deep motivation/belief/attachment to the job

Khanka (2012) further enlists the detailed elements of entrepreneurial competence and commitment which are given below:

- Detailed components of competence:

    o   Technical Skills

    o   Basic Operational Information

    o   Business Knowledge

    o   Communication Skills

    o   Interpersonal Skills

    o   Leadership Quality

    o   Team spirit and Team Building Skills

    o   Decision-Making Skills

    o   Time Management Skills

    o   Work-Coordination Skills

- Components of commitment:

    o   Self-Belief and Confidence

    o   Motivation

    o   Hardworking Spirit, Honesty, and Integrity

    o   Dedication and Determination

    o   Positive Attitude

    o   Winning Attitude

    o   Learning Attitude

    o   Perseverance

    o   Enterprising Nature

    o   Result Oriented

Above discussed components are the contributors to superior performance and if an entrepreneur wants to succeed in his venture, s/he has to work on the acquisition of all the above components of entrepreneurial competency.

1.6.2 Traits of Entrepreneurs

Starting your own business is exciting yet challenging. Besides having the right expertise, you also need to have the right mindset to face the highs and the lows that come with running your own business. Whether you wonder if you have what it takes to start your own business, or you are an experienced business owner looking to expand your skill set, you should review these essential traits of entrepreneurs that help guide success.

Here are some qualities that make an entrepreneur:

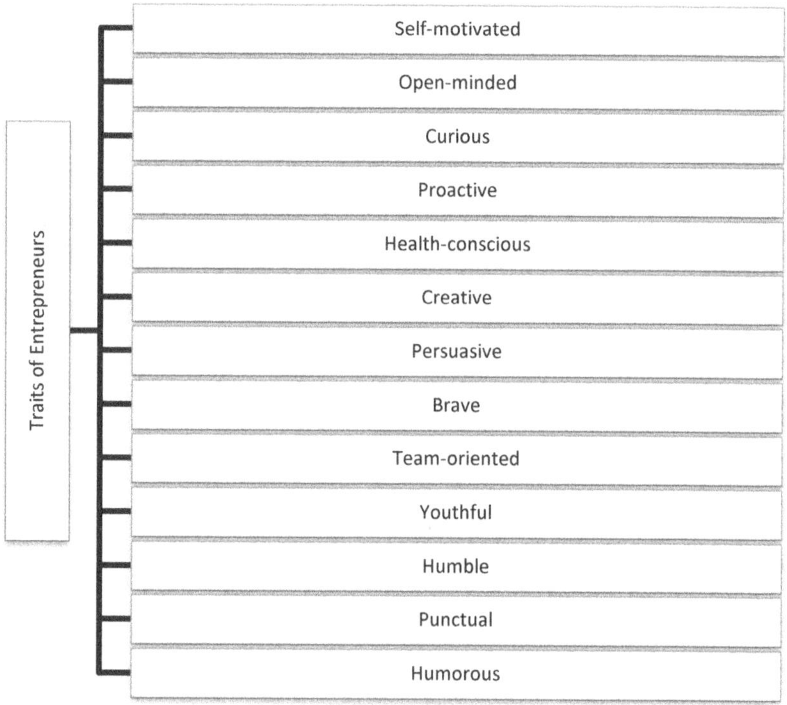

1. Self-motivated

Self-motivated describes someone who can motivate themselves rather than relying on another person. Self-motivated individuals use discipline and passion to complete essential tasks on time, limiting procrastination and producing results. Entrepreneurs must have a level of self-motivation to overcome challenges and keep up with their business practices.

For example, an entrepreneur might use their self-motivation to send out emails to clients after having a challenging client experience that resulted in a loss of business.

2. Open-minded

Someone open-minded is willing to accept or learn about new ideas and opportunities. That's why open-mindedness is such an essential trait for an entrepreneur. If they remain open to new business opportunities, they could find success in a completely different way.

For example, an entrepreneur starts a workout app company wherein gym-goers can connect with personal trainers. This idea proves unsuccessful, and so they try to start a social media advertising consultant firm. This business idea helps generate over $5,000 in revenue during the first two months of operation. Open-mindedness could mean finding success in an area you didn't want to consider.

3. Curious

Similar to open-mindedness, entrepreneurs should also have high levels of curiosity. A curious mind can produce unique and innovative ideas that provide solutions to save a start-up company.

For example, an entrepreneur creates an online recruiting network that allows companies and recruitment agencies to connect with qualified job candidates. They wonder if business would improve by marketing their site toward colleges and universities with career center services for upcoming graduates. This idea helps jumpstart site revenue while also creating a primary customer base.

4. Proactive

When an entrepreneur is proactive, they cannot only anticipate change but also take pre-emptive measures that help them conquer those changes. For example, a self-employed HR consultant creates their online course and eBook to predict a rise in competition across the industry.

5. Health-conscious

Entrepreneurs tend to lead healthy, balanced lifestyles so they can have the energy to operate their business ventures. For example, an entrepreneur might make a point to work out every morning, or they might take a day off to recharge after a long work week.

6. Creative

Another trait of entrepreneurs is creativity. Regardless of their business's industry, they have to come up with new ideas and solutions to guide their company forward. For example, an entrepreneur comes up with a unique marketing idea where they record a video series about entrepreneurship to drive traffic to their website.

7. Persuasive

Entrepreneurs should have a level of persuasiveness to convince investors to donate funds and to persuade customers to buy their products or services. For example, an entrepreneur prepares a presentation to give to potential investors about their projections for the company's growth within the next five years.

8. Brave

Bravery is another entrepreneurial trait from which you can benefit. Entrepreneurs regularly take risks from the moment they decide to start their business, and they must have the courage to accept criticism. For example, an entrepreneur puts in their two-week notice at their nine-to-five job before operating their start-up full-time.

9. Team-oriented

Entrepreneurs might start as sole proprietors, but with the right business tactics, they could soon have several employees working under them. That is why it is so crucial for entrepreneurs to be team-oriented.

For example, an entrepreneur takes on three other employees to help with sales calls and content creation. They hold daily meetings, listen to their employees' concerns, and involve them in decisions.

10. Youthful

Regardless of age, entrepreneurs should have a young perspective to keep evolving their business and combat working odd hours. For example, an entrepreneur spends the evening after meeting with clients all day to work on a new software application.

11. Humble

Entrepreneurs typically have a humble attitude because they understand the work that goes into creating and maintaining a successful business and how success can drop. For example, a successful entrepreneur makes a point to respect others and show gratitude for their business.

12. Punctual

Another excellent trait for entrepreneurs is showing up early to meetings and events. For example, an entrepreneur arrives 20 minutes early to a lunch meeting with a prospective client.

13. Humorous

Humorous entrepreneurs can laugh at their mistakes and move on from them. For example, when an entrepreneur sends an email addressed to the wrong client, they remedy the situation by sending a second response before getting back to work.

1.7 Factors Affecting Entrepreneurship Development

Entrepreneurship has significantly and positively contributed to the development of many regions of the globe. It reduces the main problems like vast unemployment, poverty reduction, heavy dependence on agriculture, and regional imbalances.

For detailed analysis, it is important to know and understand every component of the business environment that may affect the functioning of an enterprise or business. These components may be internal to entrepreneurs or external. Factors that affect entrepreneurship growth are divided into various groups so that strategies according to each group of factors can be devised. These factors are classified into the following categories/ groups:

All the factors listed above are interconnected and mutually dependent on each other. No single factor can facilitate the complete growth of entrepreneurship. For the effective functioning and speedier growth of entrepreneurship, all the factors must contribute positively.

Let us discuss each factor in detail and try to understand their implications in the emergence and growth of entrepreneurship.

1.7.1 Economic Factors

Economic factors are those which contribute to the economic development of the economy. From an economic point of view, these factors create a conducive environment for the economic development of the country and also account for the establishment and development of entrepreneurship. These factors provide economic security and a favorable environment for an enterprise. Some of the major economic factors that affect entrepreneurship growth are discussed as follows:

1.7.1.1 Capital

Capital or finance is the lifeblood of any enterprise or business and one of the major prerequisites to start an entrepreneurial activity. Without capital, entrepreneurs can never think to initiate their business. Availability of capital helps an entrepreneur to arrange the basic means of business i.e. land, machinery, material, manpower, etc. Without adequate capital, no one can combine all the means of production. Supply of adequate capital also assists in generating or increasing capital and profits. The supply of adequate capital is regarded as a lubricant to drive the engine of entrepreneurship growth. Research suggests that as the supply of capital increases, entrepreneurship also increases and this has been already experienced in entrepreneurial societies like the USA, China, Russia, and France. Researches further suggest that one of the major reasons for an entrepreneur's failure is the lack of sufficient capital in many parts of the world.

1.7.1.2 Labor

The famous economist Adam Smith has considered labor as an important factor for economic development. The availability of quality labor in the right quantity is always considered one of the major factors of economic as well as entrepreneurship development. Cheap labor is another requisite of entrepreneurship growth as it directly affects the emergence of entrepreneurship. The availability of low-cost labor is a boost for entrepreneurs as it is directly linked with the smooth functioning and profits of an enterprise. Labor problems affect the high labor-intensive enterprises but entrepreneurs can manage the impacts of this problem by bringing labor-saving innovations or through technology like Japan and the USA did to solve the problems of their industries. Labor issues can be better managed than capital issues.

1.7.1.3 Raw Material

Another factor under economic factors that affect the growth of entrepreneurship is the necessity of quality raw materials at an economic cost. To establish an enterprise in any region, the availability of raw materials is a major determinant. In the absence of raw materials, neither entrepreneurship developed nor entrepreneurs emerged. For example, if an entrepreneur wants to start a furniture house, he arranges capital through private investment and borrowings from family, and also arranges skilled labor, but, if there is no timber available in nearby markets, all efforts will go in vain. Entrepreneurs must understand the relevance of the availability of raw materials as it directly affects the cost of production. Raw materials supply does not hamper the growth of entrepreneurship as entrepreneurs can manage the problems of supply of raw materials through innovative supply chain systems and application of effective technology. If the supply of raw materials is regular in the market, then there is no need to put extra effort into the growth of the enterprise.

1.7.1.4 Market

It is the market that provides the potential reward to the entrepreneurs. The market consists of producers and buyers or a place where the seller sells his/her products to customers. The market is a major determinant for the success of any entrepreneurial initiative and without a market, no one can survive in the world of entrepreneurship. Entrepreneurs can generate capital, arrange labor, and procure raw materials but they cannot create a market, they can only generate demand for their products. Consumption of final products rests on the demand of the customers. Market size and composition of market influence the behavior of entrepreneurs. Nature, size, and composition of the market especially the dominance of a product in a given market more influential for the growth of entrepreneurship. Distance of the market from enterprises also affects the functioning of enterprises but entrepreneurs through effective transportation can manage the challenges thrown by distance issues. There are many examples where we can see that rapid development of the market significantly increases the appearance of entrepreneurs like in the German and Japanese economy.

1.7.2 Social Factors

Social scientists support that economic factors alone are not sufficient to boost entrepreneurship in any region. An entrepreneur can never be successful where society fails. Advocates of social theory state that the influence of economic factors on entrepreneurship growth depends on social factors. Some of the social factors that affect entrepreneurship growth are discussed here:

1.7.2.1 Entrepreneurship Legitimacy

For entrepreneurship establishment and growth, a system of norms and values within a social setting are major social determinants. The system of social norms and values is known as the *legitimacy of entrepreneurship*. Approval and rejection of society in terms of norms and values influence the entrepreneur's behavior. Schumpeter; a famous economist, describes these social norms and values as an appropriate social climate for entrepreneurship development. Various academicians propounded that to be a successful entrepreneur, social support is a must. The social status of entrepreneurs is considered the most important among entrepreneurship legitimacy. For entrepreneurship growth, social norms and values may be adapted or changed. Entrepreneurship legitimacy may affect or disturb the appearance of entrepreneurship but not eliminate it. Environment where legitimacy is very low but government support is very high, entrepreneurship growth may be experienced.

1.7.2.2 Social Mobility

Entrepreneurship growth also depends on social mobility. Social mobility includes both social as well as geographical mobility. Openness and flexibility in the social and cultural system affect entrepreneurship growth. Some academicians advocate that entrepreneurs grow in a flexible and liberal society where society adapts itself according to the changing environment. There are many examples where it is proved that to movement of young and educated males from a region results in the growth of entrepreneurship after their return.

1.7.2.3 Social Marginality

Sometimes entrepreneurship growth also depends on social marginality. Social marginality means a group of society supports a particular role for an individual due to differences from main social groups. An economy sees growth of entrepreneurship where a particular social system expects an individual to assume entrepreneurial roles. This marginality may be due to religious, cultural, and migration issues, etc. Social marginality is determined by entrepreneurship legitimacy and social mobility. There as examples that explain that where entrepreneurial legitimacy is low individuals are mobilized towards non-entrepreneurial roles and if legitimacy is high, mainstream individuals will assume entrepreneurial roles. Various factors contribute to social marginality which ultimately results in entrepreneurial growth. For example, one is the presence of a positive attitude toward a particular profession or business within the social group and another is a very high degree of unity or solidarity within the social group.

1.7.2.4 Security

Entrepreneurs' social and economic security also affects entrepreneurship growth. Entrepreneurs emerged in that society which provides security to him/her. Many scholars advocate that entrepreneurs' security is an important facilitator of entrepreneurship growth. It is not decisive what is the appropriate level or amount of security that results in entrepreneurial emergence. Few said a little bit of security is enough while others advocate moderate security. Few others propound that entrepreneurs emerged in turbulent conditions because sometimes it positively contributes. However, security is regarded significant factor for entrepreneurial growth. This is also justifiable as entrepreneurs are afraid of losing their assets and they expect an amount of security for their survival and where they get, entrepreneurship emerges in that society.

1.7.3 Psychological Factors

Along with economic and social factors psychological factors also contribute to the growth of entrepreneurship. If an economy provides the best economic environment and society also supports entrepreneurial endeavors but, if individuals are not self-motivated then all economic and social support will be wasted. Various psychological theories of entrepreneurship propounded that for entrepreneurship development positive attitude and motivation are crucial. The following are the psychological factors that affect entrepreneurial growth:

1.7.3.1 Motivation for high achievement

According to D. McClelland's theory of need achievement, primarily, motivation for high achievement is the major psychological determinant for entrepreneurship development. This theory advocates that entrepreneurship emerges in a society that reflects the need for achievement. A society that has a high need for achievement would expect high growth in entrepreneurship. McClelland further states that due to the need for high achievement one succeeds and the other fails in entrepreneurship due to low motivation. Further, it is suggested that the need or motivation for high achievement can be developed through training.

1.7.3.2 Status Respect

Status respect is another psychological factor that affects entrepreneurship growth. Academicians stated that withdrawal of expected status respect forces groups of society or individuals to opt for something different or unique to get the status respect and most of the time to express, dissatisfied individuals opt for entrepreneurship. Hagen (1962) supports this fact through the example of Japan's development. He stated that Japan experienced high growth in entrepreneurship due to the withdrawal of status respect from colonial rule and the Samurai group which forced Japan's society to increase innovation and creativity. Withdrawal of status respect may be due to:

- Social groups displaced from their origin.

- Values of social groups may be disrespected.

- Status respect inconsistency.

- Migration into a new society.

1.7.4 Government/Political Approach

All the above-discussed economic, social, and psychological factors are directly or indirectly influenced by the actions of the government. To achieve the developmental objectives, the government through its various policy initiatives (which are discussed in module 15) tries to provide a congenial environment to entrepreneurs. These policy measures may be in the form of economic policies, social schemes, and various training programs. The government can facilitate the establishment and growth of entrepreneurship by creating basic facilities and services for entrepreneurship. Entrepreneurial growth is affected by various government actions such as the development of special economic zones, industrial areas, industrial estates, and favourable policy initiatives. In India, government is trying to provide favourable entrepreneurial environment by enacting MSMED Act 2006, establishing separate ministry for MSME sector and by launching various attractive schemes for entrepreneurs. If government is not active or least interested in the economic development of society, no growth in entrepreneurship will be there. Other factors are also influenced by the government actions and approaches towards entrepreneurship development.

1.7.5 Other Factors

Besides economic, social, psychological, and government/political factors, there are many other factors that affect the emergence and development of entrepreneurship. Few of them are discussed below:

1.7.5.1 Infrastructural Development

Ultimate goal of development is to provide the benefits to the last citizen of the country. Most of the times, economic factors are favourable for entrepreneurship, society also adapts the environment, and government policies are also attractive but poor infrastructure for the business negatively influences the psychology of the entrepreneur. Sound infrastructural development may nullify the problems of location in many cases. Infrastructural facilities create positive way for small enterprises growth whether that is artisans or agri-entrepreneurs. Infrastructural programme coordinated with other element may gear up the growth of entrepreneurship. For example; there is a small horticulturist in a hilly town and totally focusing on the development of horticulture produces but there is no cold store or warehouse to stock the produces, in such case, slowly few small entrepreneurs may leave their business which is their choice. But, in this case, if proper warehouse or cold store is developed, this will boost the growth of such kind of enterprises.

1.7.5.2 Environmental Scanning

Another factor that affects the development of entrepreneurship is integrated approach of environmental analysis. Key to growth of entrepreneurship is effective analysis or careful research of surrounding environment. Environmental scanning gives the idea of enterprise's strengths & weaknesses and opportunities and threats posed by environment. It gives the clear idea about the target and beneficiary customers, their activities, needs, and shopping habits. Most of the times, entrepreneurs fail due to poor analysis of environment which results in slow growth of entrepreneurship.

1.7.5.3 Training

For the proper and speedier growth of entrepreneurship, entrepreneurs should have the necessary and adequate knowledge and skills to run the enterprise. Most of the entrepreneurship initiatives fail due to poor knowledge and ineffective implementation of idea. Other reason for failure or slow growth rate of entrepreneurship establishment is lack of skills. All these components are not permanent and out of control, these can be solved through proper education and training. Training significantly contributes in the establishment and development of entrepreneurship as it imparts necessary knowledge and skills to entrepreneurs for the smooth operations of the business. Proper training institutes and training programmes boost entrepreneurs to initiate entrepreneurial activity and positively influence their psychology. Moreover, training also helps in creating high need for achievement. Training further motivates entrepreneurs to take initiative and also helps in acquiring necessary competencies to achieve success in business.

1.8 Entrepreneurial Motivation (Mc Clellend's Achievements Motivation Theory)

According to McClelland, entrepreneurs do things in a new and better way and make decisions under uncertainty. Entrepreneurs are characterized by a need for achievement or an achievement orientation, which is a drive to excel, advanced, and grows.

1.8.1 Entrepreneurial Motivation

Entrepreneur is human being who has his dignity, self-respect, values, sentiments, aspirations, dreams apart from economic status. Indeed, economic betterment and social upliftment motivates a person to distinguish from others. Entrepreneurship is to a great extent the product of motivation. Motivation refers to the inner drive that ignites and sustains behaviour to satisfy needs. Behaviour is always caused and it is not spontaneous. In other words, human behaviour is goal directed or directed towards satisfaction of needs. A person's behaviour is shaped by several sociopsychological factors such as his goals, education level, cultural background, work experience, etc. When a person, feels some need tension arises in his mind until the need is satisfied. The tension motivates him to take action. If the action is successful need is satisfied otherwise the person changes the action until the need satisfaction occurs.

1.8.2 Concept of Motivation

The term 'motivation' has its origin in the Latin word "movere" which means to "move". Thus, motivation stands for movement. One can get a donkey to move by using a "Carrot or a stick", with people one can use incentives, or threats or reprimands. However, these only have a limited effect. These work for a while and then need to be repeated, increased or reinforced to secure further movement. The term motivation may be defined as "the managerial function of ascertaining the motives of subordinates and helping them to realise those motives."

1.8.3 Theories of Motivation

The importance of motivation to human life and work can be judged by the number of theories that have been propounded to explain human's behaviour. They explain human motivation through human needs and human nature.

1.8.3.1 Maslow's Need Hierarchy Theory

Prof A. H. Maslow developed a theoretical framework for understanding human motivation which has been widely acclaimed. According to him, a person's effectiveness is a function of matching his opportunity with the appropriate position of hierarchy of needs. Process of motivation begins with an assumption that behaviour, at least in part, is directed towards the satisfaction of needs.

(i) Basic Physiological Needs: The physiological needs relate to the survival and maintenance of human life. These needs include such things as food, clothing, air, water and other necessaries of life which are biological in nature. These needs are primary needs.

(ii) Safety and Security Needs: After satisfying the 'physiological needs, people want the assurance of maintaining a given, economic level. They want job security, personal bodily security, security of source of income, provision for old age, insurance - against risks, etc.

(iii) Social Needs: Man is a social being. He is, therefore, interested in conversation, sociability, exchange of feelings and grievances; companionship, recognition, belongingness, etc.

(iv) Esteem and Status Needs: These needs embrace such things as self- confidence, independence, achievement, competence, knowledge and success. These needs boost the ego of individual. They are also known as egoistic needs. They are concerned with prestige and status of the individual.

(v) Self-Fulfilment Needs: The final step under the need priority model is the need for self-fulfilment or the need to fulfil what a person considers to be his mission in life. It involves realizing one's potentialities for continued self-development and for being creative in the broadest sense of the word. After his other needs are fulfilled, a man has the desire for personal achievement.

1.8.3.2 Appraisal of Need Hierarchy Model

The need priority model may not be applied at all times in all places. Surveys in continental European countries and Japan have shown that the model does not apply very well to their managers. Their degrees of satisfaction of needed does not vary according to the need priority model. For example, workers in Spain and Belgium felt that their esteem needs are better satisfied than their security and social needs, apparently, cultural differences are an important cause of these differences. Thus, need hierarchy may not follow the sequence postulated by Maslow. Even if safety need is not satisfied, the egoistic or social need may emerge.

1.8.3.3 McClelland's Acquired Needs Theory

Each person tends to develop certain motivational drives as a result of his cognitive pattern and the environment in which he lives. David McClelland gave a model of motivation which is based on three types of needs, namely, achievement, power and affiliation. They are as follows:

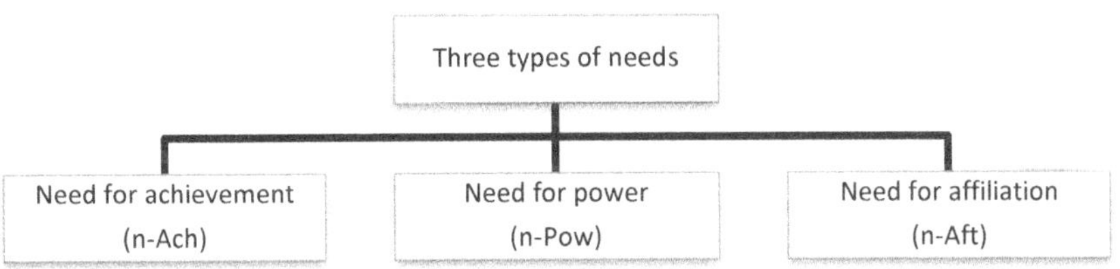

*(i) **Need for achievement (n-Ach):*** a drive to excel, advance and grow;

*(ii) **Need for power (n-Pow):*** A drive to influencing others and situations;

*(iii) **Need for affiliation (n-Aft):*** A drive for friendly and close interpersonal relationships. McClelland also suggests that these three needs may simultaneously be acting on an individual. But, in case of an entrepreneur, the high need for achievement is found dominating one.

In his view, the people with high need for achievement are characterised by the following:

(i) They set moderate, realistic and attainable goals for them.

(ii) Prefer to situations in which they can find solutions for solving personal responsibility.

(iii) They need concrete feedback on how well they are doing.

(iv) They have need for achievement for attaining personal accomplishment.

(v) They look for challenging tasks. Entrepreneurial motivation may be defined as a set of motives such as high need to achieve, moderate need for power and low affiliation motive which induce people to set up and run their own enterprises. Apart from these, entrepreneurs have other behavioural dimensions such as, tolerance for ambiguity, problem solving, creativity, etc.

1.8.4 Motives for Starting Enterprises

Several researchers have carried out research studies to identify the factors that motivate people to start business enterprises. The findings of some of the studies are as follows.

1. In this pioneering study, R.A. Sharma classified all the factors motivating the entrepreneurs into two types as follows:

(i) Internal factors

    (a) Educational background

    (b) Occupational experience

    (c) Desire to do something pioneering and innovative

    (d) Desire to be free and independent

    (e) Family background

(ii) External factors

    (a) Assistance from Government

    (b) Financial assistance from institutions

(c) Availability of technology and/or raw materials

(d) Encouragement from big business units

(e) Heavy demand for product

2. Study by Murthy, Sekhar and Rao on entrepreneurial motivation classified the factors behind entrepreneurial growth into three categories as follows:

(i) Entrepreneurial ambitions

(a) To make money

(b) To continue family business

(c) To secure self-employment/independent living

(d) To fulfil desire of self/wife/parents

(e) To gain social prestige

(f) Other ambitions-making of a decent living, self-employment of children, desire to do something creative, provide employment to others.

(ii). Compelling reasons

(a) Unemployment

(b) Dissatisfaction with the job so far held or occupation pursued

(c) Make use of idle funds

(d) Make use of technical/professional skills.

(e) Others-maintenance of large families, revival of sick unit started by father.

(iii) Facilitating factors

(a) Success stories of entrepreneurs

(b) Previous association (experience in the same or other line of activity)

(c) Previous employment in the same or other line of activity

(d) Property inherited/self-acquired/wife's

(e) Advice or influence (encouragement) of family members/ relatives/mends.

(f) Others- association as apprentices and sleeping partners.

1.8.5 The Achievement Motivation

David McClelland has developed an Achievement Motivation Theory. According to this theory an individual's Need for achievement (n-Ach) refers to the need for personal accomplishment. It is the drive to excel, to strive for success and to achieve in relations to a set of standards. The following psychological factors contribute to entrepreneurial motivation:

1. Need for achievement through self-study, goal-setting and interpersonal, support.

2. Keen interest in situations involving moderate risk.

3. Desire for taking personal responsibility.

4. Concrete measures of task performance.

5. Anticipation of future possibilities.

6. Energetic or novel instrumental activity.

7. Organisational skills, etc.

   Findings McClelland concluded that:

- Those participating in the programme displayed a more active business behaviour (51 per cent as against 25 per cent in the control group) and worked longer hours.

- Caste, traditional beliefs or western ways of life did not determine the mental makeup of a participant.

- The training as was given at Hyderabad is likely to improve those who have a great yearning to do something and have the opportunity to do so in their business framework.

1.9 Conceptual Model of Entrepreneurship

Entrepreneurship is described as a dimension of strategic posture represented by a firm's risk-taking propensity, tendency to act in competitively aggressive, proactive manners, and reliance on frequent and extensive product innovation. The proposed model delineates the antecedents and consequences of an entrepreneurial posture as well as the variables that moderate the relationship between entrepreneurial posture and firm performance. The advantages of a firm-behavior perspective on entrepreneurship are discussed, as are the theoretical and managerial implications of such a perspective.

Entrepreneurship is described as the process of handling:

- Economic activity

- Undertaking risk

- Creating something new

- Organising

- Coordinating resources

John Kao thinks you need to play on the job. "When people use the word play in a business context, it sounds kind of frivolous, but being playful is very much the source of new ideas," says Kao, author of Innovation Nation and chairman of the global Institute for Large Scale Innovation.

John Kao has developed a conceptual model of entrepreneurship in his article: Entrepreneurship, creativity and organisation in 1989. This model has four main aspects:

1. Entrepreneurial Personality: The overall success of a new venture largely depends upon the skill, qualities, traits and determination of the entrepreneur.

2. Entrepreneurial Task: It is a role played by entrepreneur in an enterprise. The major task of the entrepreneur is to recognize and exploit opportunities.

3. Entrepreneurial Environment: It involves the availability of resources, infrastructure, competitive pressures, social values, rules and regulations, stage of technology etc.

4. Organisational Context: It is the immediate setting in which creative and entrepreneurial work takes place. It involves the structure, rules, policies, culture, human resource system, communication system.

According to Kao, the most successful entrepreneur is one who adapts himself to the changing needs of the environment and makes it hospitable for the growth of his business enterprise. This ECO (Entrepreneurship, creativity ad organization) analysis frame work developed and conceptualized by John J. Kao contributes a great deal to the emergence as well as sustenance of entrepreneurship and entrepreneurial talent in the prevailing business environment.

1.10 Comparison of Entrepreneurs and Entrepreneurs

Here's a comparison of entrepreneurs and entrepreneurs in table format:

Aspect	Entrepreneur	Entrepreneur
Definition	Starts and operates a new business venture	Behaves like an entrepreneur within an organization
Independence	Operates independently	Operates within the framework of the organization

Risk	Bears significant personal risk	Faces professional risk within the organization
Autonomy	Has full autonomy and control	Has some degree of autonomy, but operates within organizational guidelines
Innovation	Driven by a desire to innovate and disrupt	Identifies opportunities for innovation within the organization
Ownership	Often retains full ownership of the venture	Does not own the initiatives developed within the organization

1.11 Comparison of Entrepreneurs and Entrepreneurship

Here's a comparison of entrepreneurs and Entrepreneurship in table format:

Aspect	Entrepreneurship	Entrepreneurship
Definition	Starting a new business venture independently	Innovating within an existing organization
Autonomy	High degree of autonomy and control	Operates within the framework of the organization
Risk	Faces significant personal risk	Risk is mitigated by the support of the organization
Examples	Steve Jobs (Apple), Elon Musk (Tesla, SpaceX)	Google's "20% time" policy, leading to Gmail, Google News

1.12 Classification of Entrepreneurs

Entrepreneurs can be classified into various categories based on different criteria. Some common classifications include:

1. ***Based on Motivation***

- ***Opportunity Entrepreneurs:*** These entrepreneurs are motivated by the desire to pursue new opportunities in the market. They are proactive in seeking and exploiting gaps or unmet needs.

- ***Necessity Entrepreneurs:*** Necessity entrepreneurs start businesses out of necessity, often due to lack of employment opportunities or financial hardship. Their primary motivation is to create income and livelihood rather than pursue opportunities.

2. ***Based on Growth Orientation:***

- ***Small Business Entrepreneurs:*** These entrepreneurs focus on starting and managing small businesses with limited growth ambitions. They often prioritize stability and lifestyle over rapid growth.

- ***Scalable or High-Growth Entrepreneurs:*** These entrepreneurs aim to build businesses that can grow rapidly and scale exponentially. They typically seek venture capital or other forms of external funding to fuel their growth.

3. ***Based on Business Stage:***

- ***Start-up Entrepreneurs:*** Start-up entrepreneurs are those who are in the early stages of building their businesses. They focus on developing and validating their business model, acquiring initial customers, and securing funding.

- ***Serial Entrepreneurs:*** Serial entrepreneurs are individuals who have started and built multiple businesses over their careers. They thrive on the process of entrepreneurship and often move from one venture to another.

4. ***Based on Industry or Sector:***

- ***Technology Entrepreneurs:*** These entrepreneurs focus on developing and commercializing technology-based products or services. They often operate in sectors such as software, hardware, biotechnology, and telecommunications.

- ***Social Entrepreneurs:*** Social entrepreneurs are driven by a mission to address social or environmental issues through innovative business solutions. They aim to create positive social impact alongside financial sustainability.

5. ***Based on Ownership Structure:***

- ***Solo Entrepreneurs:*** Solo entrepreneurs are individuals who start and run their businesses alone, without partners or co-founders.

- ***Co-Founders or Team Entrepreneurs:*** These entrepreneurs start businesses with partners or co-founders. They leverage complementary skills and expertise to build and grow their ventures.

6. ***Based on Risk Appetite:***

- ***High-Risk Entrepreneurs:*** These entrepreneurs are comfortable taking significant risks in pursuit of high rewards. They often pursue disruptive innovations or enter highly competitive markets.

- ***Low-Risk Entrepreneurs:*** Low-risk entrepreneurs are more conservative and cautious in their approach. They prefer to mitigate risks and focus on building businesses with steady, predictable growth.

1.3 Entrepreneurial Development Programmes

Entrepreneurship Development Programme (EDP) is a programme which helps in developing entrepreneurial abilities. The skills that are required to run a business successfully is developed among the students through this programme. Sometimes, students may have skills but it requires polishing and incubation. This programme is perfect for them. This programme consists of a structured training process to develop an individual as an entrepreneur. It helps the person to acquire skills and necessary capabilities to play the role of an entrepreneur effectively.

EDP is an effort of converting a person to an entrepreneur by passing him through thoroughly structured training. An entrepreneur is required to respond appropriately to the market and he/she is also required to understand the business needs. The skills needed are varied and they need to be taken care in the best possible way. EDP is not just a training programme but it is a complete process to make the possible transformation of an individual into an entrepreneur. This programme also guides the individuals on how to start the business and effective ways to sustain it successfully.

1.3.1 Objectives of Entrepreneurship Development Programme (EDP)

The objective of this programme is to motivate an individual to choose the entrepreneurship as a career and to prepare the person to exploit the market opportunities for own business successfully.

These objectives can be set both in the short-term and long-term basis.

Short-term objectives: These objectives can be achieved immediately. In the short-term, the individuals are trained to be an entrepreneur and made competent enough to scan the existing market situation and environment. The person, who would be the future entrepreneur, should first set the goal as an entrepreneur. The information related to the existing rules and regulations is essential at this stage.

Long-term objectives: The ultimate objective is that the trained individuals successfully establish their own business and they should be equipped with all the required skills to run their business smoothly.

1.3.2 Roles of EDP

An Entrepreneurship Development Programme primarily plays four roles to help an individual to become an entrepreneur. They are:

Stimulatory Role: It aims at influencing people in large number to be the entrepreneur.

This includes:

- developing managerial, technical, financial, and marketing skill

- inculcating personality traits

- promotes and reforms entrepreneurial behavior and values

- identifying a potential entrepreneur applying scientific methods

- motivational training and building a proper attitude

- strengthening the motive of a person and giving recognition

- the valuable know-how of the local products and the processes help in the selection of products, preparation of project reports

Supportive Role: It helps in the following ways:

- registration of the business

- procurement of fund

- Incubation support

- Team building and team development support

- Mentorship and guidance from industry experts

- Providing tax relief, subsidy, government schemes etc.

- guidance in product marketing

Sustaining Role: It aims at providing an effective safeguard to businesses to sustain against the cut-throat market competition. This includes:

- help in modernization, expansion, and diversification

- additional financing for further development

- Global Networking Opportunities

- creating new marketing processes

- helping access to improved services and co-working centers

Socio-economic Role: It aims at upgrading the socio-economic status of the public and includes:

- identifying entrepreneurial qualities in practicality

- creating employment opportunities in micro, small, and medium industries on an immediate basis

- arresting concentration of industries by supporting regional development in a balanced manner

- channelizing the latent resources for building an enterprise

1.3. Entrepreneurship Development Programmes in India

In India, the government has been proactive in fostering an entrepreneurial ecosystem through various initiatives. The Small Industry Services Institute (SISl), in collaboration with the Industrial Development Bank of India (IDBI), the Small Industry Development Organization (SIDO), and Technical Consultancy Organizations (TCOs), has launched Entrepreneurship Development Programmes (EDPs) to equip individuals with the necessary skills and knowledge to start and run successful businesses.

Here are a few of the most noteworthy EDPs in India:

1. Industrial Motivation Campaigns (IMCs)

It is a two-day initiative to identify and inspire individuals to embark on the entrepreneurial journey, specifically through establishing a Mid-Sized Enterprise (MSE).

2. Entrepreneurship Awareness Programmes (EAPs)

These programmes aim to educate and engage the youth about entrepreneurship and are conducted in ITIs, Polytechnics, and other technical institutions. The curriculum is designed to encompass the various aspects of industrial activity, including project profile preparation, marketing, pricing, export opportunities, financial management, and accounting.

3. Entrepreneurship-cum-Skill Development Programme (E-SDP)

It is an intensive training programme that provides a comprehensive upskilling experience for prospective entrepreneurs, the existing workforce, and technicians of MSEs. The programmes are specifically tailored to the needs of socially disadvantaged groups (SC/ST, PH, and women) and are conducted in various regions across the country, including less developed areas.

4. Management Development Programmes (MDPs)

These are short-duration training programmes aimed at enhancing the decision-making abilities of existing, aspiring, and potential entrepreneurs, resulting in improved productivity, efficiency, and profitability. The curriculum is industry-driven and can be customised to meet the unique needs of the attendees.

Exercise

1. Why entrepreneurship is considered important for economic development, job creation, and innovation?

2. Discuss the scope of entrepreneurship and the diverse opportunities it offers for individuals and societies.

3. What are the key competencies and traits that successful entrepreneurs possess, and how do they contribute to entrepreneurial success?

4.   How do government policies, regulations, and support programs impact the growth and sustainability of entrepreneurial ventures?

5.   Explain McClelland's Achievement Motivation Theory and its relevance to understanding entrepreneurial motivation.

6.   How does the need for achievement, affiliation, and power influence individuals' decision to pursue entrepreneurship?

7.   How does the entrepreneurial process differ from traditional business management, and what are the key stages involved in starting and growing a new venture?

8.   Compare and contrast the roles and characteristics of entrepreneurs and entrepreneurs within organizations.

9.   Discuss the classification of entrepreneurs based on various criteria such as scale of operations, innovation orientation, and motivation.

10.   Can you identify and describe some examples of entrepreneurial development programs and initiatives implemented at the local, national, and international levels?

Unit – 2

Entrepreneurial Idea and Innovation

Entrepreneurial Idea and Innovation: Introduction to Innovation, Entrepreneurial Idea Generation and Identifying Business Opportunities, Management skills for Entrepreneurs and managing for Value Creation, Creating and Sustaining Enterprising Model & Organizational Effectiveness.

2.1 Entrepreneurial Idea and Innovation

An "Entrepreneurial Idea" refers to a concept or proposal for a new business venture or project that is innovative, potentially profitable, and addresses a specific need or problem in the market. It is the initial spark of creativity that entrepreneurs develop into a viable business opportunity.

Entrepreneurial ideas can come from various sources, including identifying gaps in the market, observing emerging trends or technologies, solving personal pain points, or recognizing unmet needs within a particular industry or community.

2.1.1 Key Characteristics of Entrepreneurial Ideas

Key characteristics of entrepreneurial ideas include:

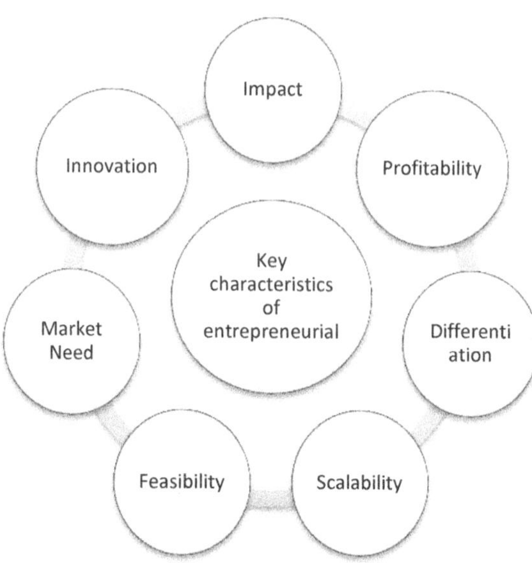

- ***Innovation:*** The idea introduces something new or offers a unique approach to solving a problem.

- ***Market Need:*** It addresses a clear need or pain point in the market, providing value to customers.

- ***Feasibility:*** The idea is technically, financially, and operationally feasible, with the potential to be implemented successfully.

- ***Scalability:*** There is potential for the business to grow and expand over time, reaching larger markets or serving additional customer segments.

- ***Profitability:*** The idea has the potential to generate revenue and achieve sustainable profitability over the long term.

- ***Differentiation:*** It offers something distinct from existing solutions or competitors, giving it a competitive advantage.

- ***Impact:*** The idea has the potential to make a positive impact on society, the environment, or specific communities.

2.1.2 Advantages and Disadvantages of Entrepreneurial Ideas

Here are some advantages and disadvantages of entrepreneurial ideas:

Advantages:

- ***Innovation:*** Entrepreneurial ideas often bring new solutions or approaches to existing problems, fostering innovation and driving progress in various industries.

- ***Potential for High Returns:*** Successful entrepreneurial ideas have the potential to generate significant profits and financial rewards for the entrepreneur and stakeholders involved.

- ***Flexibility and Autonomy:*** Entrepreneurs have the freedom to pursue their entrepreneurial ideas and shape their businesses according to their vision and values, offering a high level of autonomy and control.

- ***Personal Fulfilment:*** Pursuing entrepreneurial ideas allows individuals to pursue their passions and interests, leading to greater personal fulfilment and satisfaction.

- ***Job Creation:*** Successful entrepreneurial ventures often create job opportunities, contributing to economic growth and development by providing employment opportunities for others.

- ***Problem-Solving:*** Entrepreneurial ideas aim to address specific needs or challenges in the market, making a positive impact on society by solving problems and improving people's lives.

Disadvantages:

- ***Uncertainty and Risk:*** Entrepreneurial ventures are inherently risky, with no guarantee of success. There is a possibility of failure, financial loss, and other setbacks associated with pursuing entrepreneurial ideas.

- ***Financial Constraints:*** Bringing entrepreneurial ideas to fruition often requires significant financial investment for research, development, marketing, and other business activities. Accessing capital can be challenging, especially for new entrepreneurs.

- ***Market Competition:*** Entrepreneurial ideas may face stiff competition from existing businesses or similar startups, making it difficult to gain market share and establish a foothold in the industry.

- ***Time and Effort:*** Successfully implementing entrepreneurial ideas requires dedication, hard work, and perseverance. Entrepreneurs may need to invest a significant amount of time and effort into their ventures, often sacrificing personal time and leisure activities.

- ***Regulatory and Legal Challenges:*** Entrepreneurs may encounter regulatory hurdles, legal complexities, and compliance issues when launching their ventures, adding to the complexity and cost of doing business.

- ***Isolation and Stress:*** Entrepreneurship can be a lonely journey, with entrepreneurs often facing isolation, stress, and burnout as they navigate the challenges and uncertainties of building their ventures.

2.2 Innovation

Business ventures have some common factors amongst themselves. But they need to have some unique selling proposition (USP) to survive. It is for arming the business with a USP that the organizations need to innovate. Innovation helps a business house to survive when the winds of change hit the market, in fact innovation fuels in the winds of change. Innovation is not just creation of new ideas/ thoughts but it is also about translating them into products/ services.

Hence Innovation can be defined as the successful exploitation of new ideas – incorporating new technology, design & best practice is the key business process that enables the businesses to compete effectively.

Innovation is something more than idea generation it is because idea has little significance till it is converted into some useful product/ services. Innovation is the process of conceptualizing an idea and then transforming that idea into a product/ service. Usually innovations are being made with a desire to overcome a need or a problem. Innovation can be at the spark of light and can also take generation of experimentations. Innovation usually make the life more comfortable for a common man – but back operation in transforming ideas into products/ services at times even take lifetime of many.

2.2.1 The characteristics of Innovations

The characteristics of Innovations are:

1. Innovations are the harbingers of change

2. Innovations can take place at the spark of light or can take generation of experiments

3. Innovations can be both revolutionary as well as extension to the existing products/ services.

4. Innovations provide a USP to a business.

5. Innovations are action oriented i.e. active and searching new ideas.

6. Innovations help in making the product, service or process simple and understandable.

7. Innovations help in making the product, service or process customer based.

8. Innovation is all about trying, testing and revising.

2.2.2 Definitions of Innovation from Different Perspectives

Innovation is a broad concept that can be defined and understood in various ways depending on the context. Here are several definitions of innovation from different perspectives:

- ***Economic Perspective:*** Innovation is the process of creating new products, services, technologies, or business models that add value to society and contribute to economic growth and development.

- ***Business Perspective:*** Innovation refers to the introduction of new ideas, products, processes, or methods that improve efficiency, productivity, competitiveness, or profitability within a business or organization.

- ***Technological Perspective:*** Innovation involves the development and application of new technologies, techniques, or systems that enable the creation of novel solutions to existing problems or opportunities.

- ***Social Perspective:*** Innovation encompasses changes in social structures, behaviours, or norms that lead to positive social outcomes, such as improved quality of life, equality, sustainability, or well-being.

- ***Cultural Perspective:*** Innovation involves the creation or adoption of new cultural practices, expressions, or artifacts that shape the way people think, interact, or perceive the world around them.

- ***Entrepreneurial Perspective:*** Innovation is the process of identifying and exploiting opportunities to create value by introducing new products, services, or business models that meet unmet needs or solve existing problems in the market.

- ***Creative Perspective:*** Innovation is the result of creative thinking, imagination, and experimentation that leads to the development of original ideas, concepts, or solutions that challenge conventional wisdom and push the boundaries of what is possible.

- ***Incremental vs. Radical Innovation:*** Innovation can be classified into incremental, where small improvements are made to existing products or processes, and radical, where entirely new and disruptive ideas or technologies are introduced.

- ***Open Innovation:*** Innovation involves collaboration and knowledge sharing across organizational boundaries, where ideas, resources, and expertise are sourced externally as well as internally to drive innovation.

- ***User-Centric Innovation:*** Innovation focuses on understanding and addressing the needs, preferences, and behaviors of end-users or customers, with the aim of creating products or services that deliver superior value and user experience.

These definitions illustrate the multifaceted nature of innovation and highlight its importance across various domains, from business and technology to society and culture. Ultimately, innovation involves creativity, vision, and the willingness to challenge the status quo to create positive change and drive progress.

2.2.3 Advantages of Innovation in Entrepreneurship:

Advantages of Innovation in Entrepreneurship are:

- ***Competitive Advantage:*** Innovative entrepreneurs can differentiate themselves from competitors by offering unique products or services that meet customer needs more effectively or efficiently.

- ***Market Leadership:*** Successful innovation can propel entrepreneurs to become market leaders, gaining a significant share of the market and establishing a strong brand presence.

- ***Increased Profitability:*** Innovation often leads to higher profitability through cost savings, increased sales, premium pricing for innovative products or services, and enhanced customer loyalty.

- ***Customer Satisfaction:*** Innovative solutions can improve the customer experience by providing better quality, convenience, or value, leading to higher levels of satisfaction and loyalty.

- ***Business Growth:*** Innovation fuels business growth by opening up new markets, attracting new customers, and expanding revenue streams. It allows entrepreneurs to scale their businesses more rapidly and sustainably.

- ***Adaptability and Resilience:*** Innovative entrepreneurs are better equipped to adapt to changing market conditions, technological advancements, and consumer preferences, making them more resilient to disruptions and uncertainties.

2.2.4 Disadvantages of Innovation in Entrepreneurship

Disadvantages of Innovation in Entrepreneurship are:

- ***High Risk:*** Innovation inherently involves uncertainty and risk, as there is no guarantee that new ideas or ventures will be successful. Failure rates for innovative ventures can be high, leading to financial loss and setback for entrepreneurs.

- ***Resource Intensive:*** Developing and implementing innovative ideas often requires significant investment of time, money, and resources. Entrepreneurs may face challenges in accessing the necessary capital, talent, and infrastructure to support their innovation efforts.

- ***Resistance to Change:*** Innovation can face resistance from customers, employees, or stakeholders who are accustomed to existing products, processes, or business models. Overcoming resistance to change can be a significant barrier to successful innovation.

- ***Regulatory and Legal Challenges:*** Innovations may encounter regulatory hurdles, compliance issues, or intellectual property disputes that can delay or hinder their implementation. Entrepreneurs must navigate complex legal and regulatory landscapes to protect their innovations and ensure compliance.

- ***Market Acceptance:*** Not all innovative ideas gain market acceptance or traction. Entrepreneurs may struggle to convince customers of the value proposition of their innovations or may face challenges in educating the market about new products or services.

- ***Cultural and Organizational Barriers:*** Innovation can be stifled by cultural norms, organizational hierarchies, or resistance to change within the entrepreneurial venture or industry. Creating a culture of innovation and fostering collaboration and creativity are essential for overcoming these barriers.

2.2.5 Entrepreneurship and Innovation

Entrepreneurship has been defined in the literature in many ways, but there are four descriptions that have become dominant in the research: the entrepreneur as an innovator (Schumpeter), as an arbitrager/creator of balance (Kirtzner), as a bearer of uncertainty (Frank Knight), and the entrepreneur as a coordinator (Jean-Baptiste Say). The main part of the later literature on the significance of entrepreneurship constitutes refinements or variants of these four main tracks.

Schumpeter's innovator is the definition that makes the most distinct connection between entrepreneurship, innovations and economic growth, and this report largely bases the continued discussion on this definition.

In terms of innovation, a common definition from OECD's Oslo manual is the following:

An 'innovation' is the implementation of a new or significantly improved product (goods or service), or process, a new marketing method, or a new organisational method in business practices, workplace organisation or external relations

Hence, it involves a change that creates new conditions for economic activity, either for individual companies, on a market or globally. A central part of the definition is that it is something new that has commercial value (implementation), in contrast to an invention that does not necessarily benefit anyone other than the inventor.

Traditionally, the term of innovation has often been linked with the development of new technology, but it is becoming increasingly clear that this restrictive view is not sufficient to explain the development that takes place with regard to the growth of new, often service-based, industries and markets.

However, from an analytical perspective, it is possible to clearly delimit what is meant by both entrepreneurial activities and innovations. An excessively broad definition is at risk of becoming meaningless. Growth Analysis' assignment involves studying the connection between entrepreneurial activities and the development of innovations, as well as how this in turn affects economic growth. The factors that can be politically influenced are of particular interest. The latter means that certain choices must be made with regard to the abundance of knowledge that exists concerning these issues. The choice made is to only focus in the empirical studies on innovation that occurs in companies and affects economic growth.

The conclusion drawn in the report is **that entrepreneurship and innovation are two very closely related phenomena in the sense that innovation requires some form of entrepreneurial behaviour.** The terms are not synonymous, however; there are reasons in some cases to make a clear distinction between them – particularly from a policy perspective.

The process from idea to innovation and growth is driven by various functions that can each be performed by different actors. **Ideas are created** by researchers, inventors or other visionary thinkers. They **are identified** by the entrepreneur, who is always a private individual, but can be found in a large, small, new or old company or in a public organisation. The function performed is, in Schumpeter's words, "getting things done", in other words converting ideas to commercial use or driving innovations forward. Commercial benefit only becomes a driver of growth, however, when the innovation becomes **wide-spread** in society through secondary innovations and imitations that lower the costs.

As an effect of the two concepts of entrepreneurship and innovation being so clearly related, **entrepreneurship should be linked to the implementation of innovative ideas, not to companies of a certain age, size, industry or region.**

2.3 Relationship between Entrepreneurship and Innovation

Table to illustrate the relationship between entrepreneurship and innovation:

Aspect	Entrepreneurship	Innovation
Definition	The process of starting and running a business or organization, typically characterized by risk-taking and innovation.	The introduction of new ideas, products, services, or processes that create value and drive positive change.
Focus	Business creation and management	Idea generation and implementation
Role	Entrepreneur identifies opportunities, takes risks, and manages resources to create value and achieve goals.	Innovator develops and implements creative solutions to address market needs or challenges.
Purpose	To exploit opportunities, solve problems, and fulfill unmet needs in the market.	To introduce new products, services, or processes that improve efficiency, effectiveness, or customer satisfaction.
Outcome	Creation of new ventures, job creation, economic growth	Development of new products, services, market disruption.

Traits	Vision, creativity, risk-taking, resilience, leadership.	Creativity, problem-solving skills, adaptability, collaboration.
Examples	Starting a new business, launching a new product or service, pursuing opportunities in emerging markets.	Developing groundbreaking technologies, implementing innovative business models, creating disruptive solutions.

2.4 Entrepreneurial Idea Generation

2.4.1 Business Opportunity Identification

Business opportunity, in general sense implies a good chance or a favourable situation to do the business. Business opportunity identification is central to the domain of entrepreneurship. Entrepreneurship revolves around answering various questions with regard to why, where, when and how business opportunities arise. Recognizing an opportunity often results from the knowledge and expertise of the individual entrepreneur. The entrepreneur must always be ready to use his knowledge and experience and turn his ideas into a powerful business opportunity and create a successful venture. Opportunity identification and are like corner stones of a business enterprise. Better the former, better is the latter. However, all the identified opportunities and the business ideas must be carefully screened and analysed by the entrepreneur. The first steps for every entrepreneur is the identification of a business opportunity and generate a new business idea. The generation of new business idea is not an easy task. Thus, let us now examine various sources and techniques of idea generation for new products and services. You need to understand that business opportunity, identification and involves a thorough research of the dynamic market.

2.4.2 Trends

Trends mean something which is trending in your target market. Trends often provide great opportunities for starting a new venture, particularly when the entrepreneur can be at the start of a trend that lasts for a considerable period of time. Seven trends that provide business opportunities are discussed below:

- **Wearable Trend:** As the cost and size of microprocessors continue to shrink; the ability to carry the computers with monitors to display relevant information is now a reality. The wearable tech industry includes categories such as body monitoring (Fitbit) which has brought smart watches into the market. Consumer's interest in smart watches is expected to boost the industry further as new companies come forward to service the industry with applications and accessories.

- **Green Trend:** The green sector continues to brimming opportunities around the world. The Green sector is filled with opportunities for entrepreneurs around the world. Today consumers are willing to pay more for green products. Going green is not going away, but the various trends within the green business movement will change direction, creating opportunities for new products and new businesses. For example: a movement towards hybrid cars, eco-friendly products and packaging etc.

- **Payments:** The dynamic payments industry continues to expand and evolve, with digital payment vehicles and transaction volumes growing across the globe. This industry includes services for lending money (lendingtree.com) to products that allow anyone to accept credit/debit cards (billdesk) as well as billing and accounting services (Paytm).

- **Maker Trend:** The maker movement is a trend in which individuals or groups of individuals create and market products that are recreated and assembled. The recreation and assembly are done by using unused, discarded or broken electronic, plastic, silicon or virtually any raw material and/or products from a computer-related device. The maker movement has led to the creation of a number of technology products and solutions by typical individuals working without supportive infrastructure. For example, MintyBoost, a popular DIY USB charger kit built uses an Altoids tin, batteries and a few connectors which can easily be created using instructions online, or purchased from other makers who sell their devices.

- ***Mobile Trend:*** The mobile phones continue to revolutionise the way of purchases and interaction with consumers. The consumers are short of time so the activities once done on desktops are now done on mobile phones or tablets. There is no point in drawing a distinction between future of technology and future of mobile. Both have been moving towards consumers friendly operations.

- ***Health Trend:*** Health maintenance concern about health care, are one of the biggest trends that will continue in the next decade as the population ages. This provides many opportunities for entrepreneurs including: Cosmetic procedures, Fitness centres (also refers as gym), Fitness toys (e.g. punch balloon, bi-cycle, etc.), Fit food, Care clinics, And wellness coaches. Green Mountain Digital is developing a social network platform for nature lovers.

- ***The Internet of Things:*** With each passing day, the population connecting to internet has been increasing. The potential for nearly everything we interact with to be connected to the internet has given rise to new products. They can access internet through an embedded WIFI transmitter. It has been assumed that internet will disappear soon, meaning that you would not even sense that you are interacting with it.

2.4.3 Good Business Idea

A business idea is a starting point for any current or future entrepreneurs. It is essential because it is the beginning of a new life for a business and an entrepreneur. An idea is important in the initial stage of a start-ups as well as their development. The results from good business ideas will feel in all Phases of the development of a firm, but will also depend on other entrepreneurial activities. Any good business ideas could be an invention, a new product or service, or an original idea or solution to an everyday problem. A good business idea does not necessarily have to be an unique product or service. Majority of the entrepreneurs becomes successful with the accomplishment as a result of the exceptional execution of ordinary ideas. The chances of success therefore will be far greater if you can market a product that is similar to existing offerings, while providing greater value to customers. In entrepreneurship 'ideas' is used as an acronym.

IDEAS stand for:

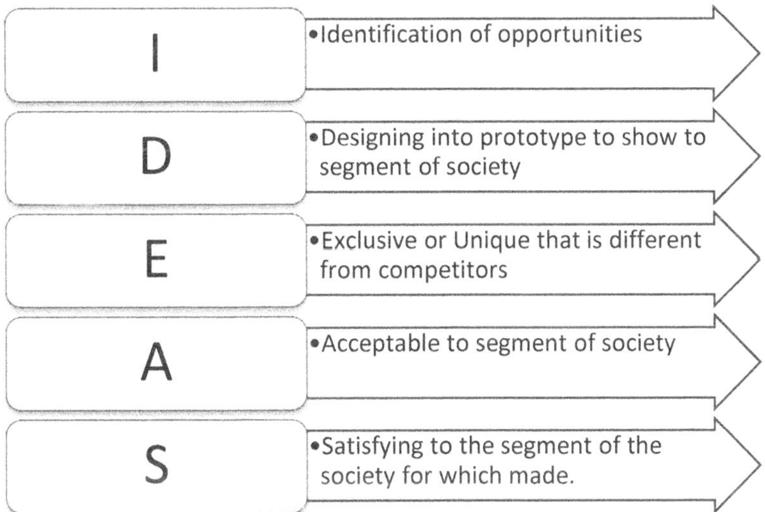

In other words, ideas are referred to as problems expressed by the people in the society. Any problem stated by the consumers becomes a business opportunity to be fulfilled by providing necessary goods or services as a solution to their problems. For example, if a person is looking for keeping his/her body fit then this problem can be solved by offering gym facility to him/her.

2.4.4 Sources of Business Ideas

Business ideas are thoughts that when implemented can lead to income generation. Coming up with new and feasible business ideas is a crucial initial step to become a great entrepreneur. Business ideas are all around us in the environment. Some of these business ideas emerge from market analysis and consumer needs, while others emerge from a long research process. Sources of new product ideas include: company employees, customers, competitors, outside inventors, acquisitions, and channel members. However, there is no conventional technique for sensing and selecting a right business opportunity; these are some of the fruitful sources of business ideas adopted by successful entrepreneurs which can be classified as internal and external sources of idea generation. Let us learn them in detail.

2.4.4.1 Internal sources

Internal sources facilitate the generation of business idea from within the organization. When people think about creativity in a business, they are often referring to ideas for new products and services that come from the employees. Using internal sources, the company can find new ideas through formal Research and Development (R&D) or through formal and informal employee's suggestions. Rewards and recognition can be provided in order to obtain maximum participation from the employees.

Research and Development: R&D can be carried out in-house or outside the organization. R&D activity suggests what and how a new or modified product can be produced to meet the customers' requirements. R&D involves researching the market and the customer needs and developing new and improved products and services to fit these needs. Businesses that have an R&D strategy have a greater chance of success than businesses that not have R&D strategy can lead to innovation and increased productivity and can boost competitive advantage of the business. However, research and development can be expensive and time-consuming process but its benefits outweigh its costs.

Entrepreneurship: An entrepreneur is a person who takes on the responsibility to innovate new ideas, products and processes or any new invention within the organization. Beyond its internal R&D process, companies can use the brains of its employees—from executives to scientists, engineers, and manufacturing staff to sales people. Many companies have developed successful "entrepreneurial" programs that encourage employees to envision and develop new-product ideas.

Hobbies and Interests: Hobbies are the activities that one enjoys doing during leisure time and can prove to be a major source of business ideas which is generated from within an entrepreneur. In fact, many successful entrepreneurs have established great successful business ventures while pursuing their interests or hobbies. Virat Kohli, one of the greatest sportsmen of the 21st century has started its own fitness centre chain named 'Chisel' and turned his interests into venture.

2.4.4.2 External Sources

Business can also obtain brilliant new-product ideas from any of a number of external sources. These external sources are numerous, such as customers, competitors, channel members, but the firms differ greatly as to where they concentrate their efforts for outside assistance and the extent to which external ideas are sought after and used.

Need Recognition of Customers: Potential entrepreneurs should always pay close attention to the needs of the people in the society. A business opportunity arises from the need which is strongly felt by a vast majority of people. When a need is strongly felt and people are unable to satisfy it themselves, they tend to find its solution from the outside world. Entrepreneurs should try to recognise this need as and make sincere efforts to turn this need into a successful business venture. Needs can be recognized by conducting surveys, whether formally or informally, through questionnaires, interviews or observation.

Existing Products and Services: Improving upon the already existing goods and services is yet another successful source of business idea generation. This improvement might result into a completely new product or service having more market appeal and sales potential. Thus, an entrepreneur should carefully analyse and evaluate existing products and services of itself and competitors and should bring out ways to improve these offerings. That is why it is said that entrepreneurs need to be creative and innovative. To understand it clearly let us take an example. Data storage was never as easy as it is now via cloud storages which were once a floppy disk. This got improved to a completely new product as CD, and then turned into a pen drive and various other small chip sized memory cards. Now data is stored on the virtual clouds like iCloud, google drive etc.

Distribution Network: Members of distribution partner like dealers, wholesalers, retailers and agents have proved to be one of the brilliant sources of new idea generation. The distribution networks have proximity with the customers and they can recognise the unsatisfied needs of the customers. No one knows more than them, what do the consumer wants and what are they getting at the moment. These channel partners can provide with a wide variety of suggestions regarding improvements in the existing products and services as well as new product ideas according to the needs of the market as they deal in number of products and services and thus might be having a maximum experience across industry.

Trade Journals, Business Magazines and Newspapers: Statistical information and other reports are being published by various trade journals, business magazines and newspapers which can be used in generating new business ideas. They write on current trends in industry, best practices, legal issues, and general business environment which can provide gainful insights while generating new business ideas for a successful new venture and its growth. For example: Laghu Udyog Samachar Magazine is a magazine published by MSME in India for identification of business ideas.

Trade Fairs and Exhibitions: Trade fairs and exhibitions have proved to be one of the excellent sources of idea generation since decades as they are usually advertised on the Internet, radio, and newspapers. People from all around the world come and participate in these fairs and exhibition displaying their new products and services.

One can meet a number of manufacturers, sales representatives, distributors, wholesalers, and franchisers who can provide gainful insights in generating new business ideas and launching a new venture.

Government Schemes: In order to eliminate unemployment and to motivate youth to become entrepreneurs rather than craving for employment, government of India has initiated various schemes to provide training and assistance to the people having a desire to start their own enterprises. These schemes by themselves, is a great source of idea generation. For instance, Khadi and Village Industries Development Board in India have led Indian handicrafts across borders by providing a variety of incentives. These incentives are provided to village craftsmen and artisans in the form of training, subsidized loans and raw materials, export promotions etc.

2.4.5 Techniques of Idea Generation

Idea generation is described as the process of creating, developing an abstract concrete or visual ideas and anyone can participate in generating new ideas. Let us learn the techniques of idea generation.

Brainstorming: Brainstorming is a creative problem-solving technique and also an informal approach to business ideas generation. It encourages people to come up with thoughts and ideas that can, at first, seem a bit crazy. The sustainable sincere effort is required for the conversion of crazy idea into real business opportunities. Some of these ideas can be crafted into original, creative solutions to a problem, while others can spark even more ideas. The objective of brainstorming is to come up with as many ideas as possible and therefore, during brainstorming sessions, there is no criticism, rewards or judgements. For more successful results, brainstorming should be conducted with the help of experts.

Brain Writing: Brain writing is an idea-generating method that involves everyone in a group activity. It is a kind of written brainstorming. Unlike brainstorming, which is verbal and where the ideas are being generated spontaneously, brain writing tends to give more time to the participants to generate ideas. Brain writing is silent technique where the group of people (usually six) are required to write minimum three ideas on special forms or cards which are circulated to each participant for a pre-specified duration.

Focus Groups: Focus groups have been used for a variety of purposes and have been widely used for idea generation. The group is lead by a moderator to conduct an in-depth discussion. The group usually consists of 8-14 recruited participants. In focus group, the role of moderator is very much important for providing direction and leading the group towards the generation of fresh ideas for new product development. For example, a focus group created by a car manufacturer to discuss about the possible improvements in the existing model of its cars. Focus groups are helpful not only in idea generation but also in idea screening.

Mind mapping: Mind maps are an idea generation strategy to produce ideas effectively by association. It is a powerful graphical technique which is used to translate whatever is running into the minds into a visual picture. The process of mind-mapping involves penning down a central theme and coming out with new and associated ideas that branch out from the central idea. These branches form a connected nodal structure. With respect to creative problem solving, mind maps help to show how are different pieces of information or different ideas connected. It helps to unlock potential of the brain.

Heuristic Ideation Technique: HIT is an idea generation technique that facilitates generation of new product ideas by exploring different products' features and making different combinations in order to search for a new product idea. Under this technique, new product ideas are developed using the combination of the elements of already existing products.

SCAMPER: SCAMPER is an activity-based thinking process that helps to generate diverse ideas. SCAMPER is an acronym which stands for: S- Substitute; C-Combine; A-Adapt; M-Modify; P-Put to another use; E- Eliminate; R-Rearrange. Substitute means thinking about substituting different parts of the product or its processing for something else. Combine means thinking about combining different products' features or processes in order to develop completely new product. Adapt signifies adapting different measures according to the situation. Modify signifies modifying features, physical qualities, size or price of existing product. Put to another use means using the existing product for some another problem or as a byproduct. Eliminate signifies eliminating non-essential components and reducing time/efforts and cost. Rearrange means rearranging the components or using different order.

Problem Inventory Analysis: Problem Inventory analysis though seems similar to focus group method, yet it is somewhat different from the latter in the sense that it not only generates the ideas, but also identifies the problems the product faces. The procedure involves two steps: One, providing consumers a list of specific problems in a general product category. Two identifying and discussing the products in the category that suffers from the specific problems. This method is found relatively more effective for the reason that it is easier to relate known products to a set of suggested problems and then arrive at a new product idea.

Free Association: Free association is a method of developing new idea through a chain or a cycle of word association. The process involves a word relating to the problem being written down, then another and another. Free association contains elements of several other idea- generating techniques and depends on a mental 'stream of consciousness' and network of associations that are of two types:

First is Serial association which starts with a trigger, you record the flow of ideas that come to mind, each idea triggering the next, ultimately reaching a potentially useful one.

The second is Centred association, (which is close to classical brainstorming) prompts you to generate multiple associations to the original trigger so that you 'delve' into a particular area of associations.

2.5 Scanning and Screening of Business Ideas

So far you have seen different sources of business ideas and techniques for generating business ideas. Ideas may be many but as an individual you may not want to make use of all the possible business ideas and to convert them into business venture. Therefore, you need to screen the ideas, evaluate each of them and select one or few that is viable. Idea screening is a process used to evaluate innovative product ideas, strategies and marketing trends. Screening is essentially an elimination technique. The purpose of idea generation is to generate large number of ideas whereas the purpose of idea screening is to reduce these numbers to some profitable business ideas. Idea screening criteria are used to determine compatibility with overall business objectives and evaluate whether the idea would offer a viable return on investment. Whatever does not meet these criteria is typically discarded. In simple words, idea screening refers to evaluating the business ideas on the basis of their profitability and discarding those which are not fruitful ones. The purpose is to eliminate the number of ideas without screening away the potential ones. The ideas can be screened based on eight criteria's and the entrepreneur must aim to answer following questions while screening ideas:

- ***Attractiveness of Idea:*** Would you enjoy doing it? For an idea to become a successful business venture, it should be attractive to the entrepreneur as well the market. No enterprise can become successful if the idea is not attractive enough to be translated into a business.

- ***Ability to undertake:*** Do you have the skills needed to do it? One can generate any number of ideas but the ideas for which the entrepreneurs have skills and abilities are considered to be the best ones. Even if the skills are not sufficient, then the entrepreneur must consider whether these skills can be developed by undertaking some training and development programmes or not.

- ***Practicality:*** Is it something that really can be done? A workable idea is one which is feasible and practical. Before committing funding to a proposed venture, one must decide whether it is viable or not.

- **_Potential Market Demand:_** Will the customers be willing to buy it? Before selecting an idea, its market demand must be carefully analysed. There is no point investing in something that cannot stimulate its demand,

- **_Ability to Combat Competition:_** Is there competition in the market and can you combat it in some way? A careful analysis of competition present in the market is necessary before resorting to an idea. One must ensure the intensity of available competition in the market. They should enter only that market where they can manage the competition and differentiate their product.

- **_Ability to Differentiate:_** Can you differentiate it in some way that can be sustained over a long period? The good idea is the one which has the ability to be sustained for over a long period of time. It has to be differentiated from those of competitors.

- **_Price Potential:_** Can you avoid competing simply on price? The competition should not be based only on price as that can lead to a price war. The price war is not appropriate for long term survival of the business.

- **_Resource Availability:_** Do you think you have, or can get the resources you need to start up the business? For conducting any business, sufficient amount of resources is required. One must ensure that they have or can gather sufficient amount of resources required for business.

2.6 New Product Development Process

Entrepreneurs need to be concerned with formally evaluating an idea throughout its evolution. Care must be taken to be sure that idea can be the basis for a new venture. This can be done through careful evaluation that results into go or no-go decision at each of the stages of the product planning and development process.

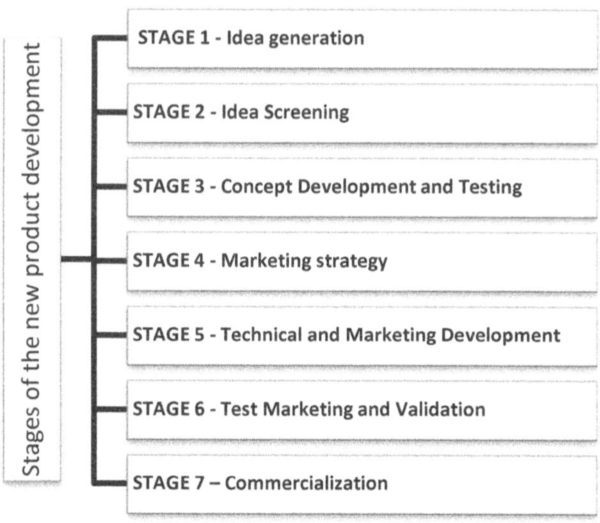

The new product development is done through following stages:

STAGE 1 - Idea generation

The new product development process starts with idea generation. Idea generation refers to the systematic search for new-product ideas. Typically, a company generates hundreds of ideas, maybe even thousands, to find a handful of good ones in the end. Two sources of new ideas can be identified:

Internal idea sources: The company finds new ideas internally. That means R&D, but also contributions from employees.

External idea sources: The company finds new ideas externally. This refers to all kinds of external sources, e.g. distributors and suppliers, but also competitors. The most important external source are customers, because the new product development process should focus on creating customer value.

Various examples exist in the market place where observations made by the entrepreneur both inside the country and outside the country with the focus on customers have helped them in idea generation.

STAGE 2 - Idea Screening

The next step in the new product development process is idea screening. Idea screening means nothing else than filtering the ideas to pick out good ones. In other words, all ideas generated are screened to spot good ones and drop poor ones as soon as possible. While the purpose of idea generation was to create a large number of ideas, the purpose of the succeeding stages is to reduce that number. The reason is that product development costs may increase substantially in the later stages. Therefore, the company would like to go ahead with only those product ideas that will turn into profitable products.

STAGE 3 - Concept Development and Testing

Today, it is increasingly common for companies to run some small concept test in a real marketing setting. The product concept is a synthesis or a description of a product idea that reflects the core element of the proposed product. Marketing tries to have the most accurate and detailed product concept possible in order to get accurate reactions from target buyers. Those reactions can then be used to inform the final product, the marketing mix, and the business analysis. New tools leveraging technology for product development are available that support the rapid development of prototypes which can be tested with potential buyers. When concept testing can include an actual product prototype, the early test results are much more reliable. Concept testing helps companies avoid investing in bad ideas and at the same time help them catch and keep outstanding product ideas.

There are various types of marketing tools that can help in concept development and testing. One such tool is conjoint analysis and it can help the marketer to arrive at a concept proved statistically and therefore truly justified. For example, manufacturer wants to introduce a coffee making machine and this machine can come in different variations based on its attributes.

When these options are before the manufacturer, he/she has to come out with that combination in case of coffee making machine that can provide the optimal solution to the customer. It can be a coffee making machine with 600 ml capacity with a brew time of 4 minutes and with the price range of Rs 1000 which can be concept 1. Similarly, concept 2 can be machine with the capacity of 800 ml with a brew time of 4 minutes and in the price range of Rs. 1000. And such concepts, once they are developed have to be tested on consumers so that the consumers' opinion may become the final verdict to be launched in the market.

STAGE 4 - Marketing strategy

At this stage, a marketing strategy will be created for the selected concept. Marketing strategy is created in three steps. These steps are:

Identify in which market will the new product concept can be sold, how much profit is targeted from new product concept and what are its planned value proposition, sales and market share for the first few years.

Identify the price at which new product concept will be sold, how it will be distributed in the market and what will be the marketing budget for the first year and so on.

Identify how much new product concept will be sold in the long term, how much profit is targeted from long-term sale and what will be long- term marketing mix strategy.

This stage is very crucial because as Napoleon said that "Wars are not won in the battle field rather on the piece of paper. Similarly, the entrepreneur is required to craft marketing strategy for the business concept finalised and then go for its implementation so that more or less the success is guaranteed." To learn more about marketing you may read our course BCOE-141 "Principles of Marketing".

STAGE 5 - Technical and Marketing Development

A product that has passed the screening and business analysis stages is ready for technical and marketing development. Technical development processes vary greatly according to the type of product. For a product with a complex manufacturing process, there is a lab phase to create specifications and an equally complex phase to develop the manufacturing process. For a service offering, there may be new processes requiring new employee skills or the delivery of new equipment. These are only two of many possible examples, but in every case the company must define both what the product is and how will it be delivered to many buyers.

While the technical development is under way, the marketing department is testing the early product with target customers to find the best possible marketing mix. Ideally, marketing uses product prototypes or early production models to understand and capture customer responses and to identify how best to present the product to the market. Through this process, product marketing must prepare a complete marketing plan—one that starts with a statement of objectives and ends with a coherent picture of product distribution, promotion, and pricing integrated into a plan of marketing action.

STAGE 6 - Test Marketing and Validation

Test marketing is the final stage before commercialization. The objective is to test all the variables in the marketing plan including elements of the product. Test marketing represents an actual launching of the total marketing program, done on a limited basis. Initial product testing and test marketing are not the same. Product testing is totally initiated by the producer. He or She selects the sample of people, provides the consumer with the test product, and offers the consumer some sort of incentive to participate. In product testing, there are two types of tests which are conducted called alpha and beta testing. In alpha testing, the product is subject to checking of the product's standards/ specifications and is done in the laboratory. In Beta testing, the product is put to test in a simulated situation. If the product passes through all the tests when the product is made available for actual use that shows that product is free from all technical problems because of which the product may fail in the market place. For example, in case of car the car is subject to alpha testing, by checking the controls on the apparatuses in the laboratory and once the whole car is ready then the speed of the car, RPM of the engine, breaking power, etc. is all an outcome of simulation test called beta testing and a sticker is placed on the car titled "PDI done" i.e. pre delivery inspection completed.

Test marketing on the other hand, is distinguished by the fact that the test group represents the full market, the consumer must make a purchase decision and pay for the product, and the test product must compete with the existing products in the actual marketing environment. For these and other reasons, a market test is an accurate simulation of the broader market and serves as a method for reducing risk. It should enhance the new product's probability of success and allow for final adjustment in the marketing mix before the product is introduced on a large scale. In case of test marketing, once the product is finalised, a small geographical area is identified for the target market and in that area the product is sampled to the consumers to use the product. After a week or so their feedback is obtained to find out the shortcomings in the product reported by the consumers. These shortcomings are then removed in the laboratory and once no further problems are expressed by the consumers at the time of using the product, it is assumed that now the product is fit for final launching and commercialization.

STAGE 7 – Commercialization

The first thing to be done at this stage is determining the time when new product concept will be commercialized or introduced to the market. Then, at which scale or capacity, new product concept will be introduced to the market formally i.e., at a small scale such as a city, medium scale such as a region, or at a big scale such as the national market, or the international market. Usually, most businesses prefer to introduce new products into the market at small or medium scales and expand the market in the process as introduction of new product at a big scale requires more capital, confidence and capacity which only few businesses have. This stage requires patience on the part of the entrepreneur and is the beginning of the recovery of the investment made by the entrepreneur in the form of return from the sale of the product.

2.7 Critical Factors of the New Venture Development

The five critical factors are explained below for the assessment of new venture:

Uniqueness: Uniqueness is something that will make your business to be the only one of its kind of business. The unique business idea is something that will increase the business potential energy of your business. It can be done by creating a USP. A unique selling proposition (USP) is a well-thought-out statement that helps a company distinguishes itself from other businesses in its category. In most instances, companies will focus on a single feature or benefit that solves a problem, satisfies a need, or takes away their customers' pain as their USP. In order to articulate it to their customer base in a memorable way, companies will create taglines or summaries of their USP and insert them into their advertising messages.

Investment: The capital investment in ever business varies considerably. In some industries only large-scale start-ups are feasible whereas in some cases only small-scale start-ups are feasible.

Growth of Sales: The pattern of growth of sales needs to be analysed in advance. The rate of growth expected also needs to be calculated to know the gestation period of the new venture to breakeven. It involves answering various questions like: Are sales and profits expected to grow slowly or level off shortly after start up? Are large profit expected at some point, with only small and moderate sales growth? Are both sales growth and profit growth

Product Availability: Availability of the product after the promotion is an essential factor to be considered. Sometimes, firms make so much hurry in launching new product but unable to make it available at the doorsteps of the target population which may tarnish its image. Sometimes the product launched during its development stage which needs further modifications or testing.

Customer Knowledge about their requirements: It is important for the entrepreneur to understand the requirement of the customer before starting the production in the venture. The product available from the venture to be started should understand the needs and wants of the consumer through market survey which will increase the likelihood of venture success. Venture risk is affected by availability of customers for start-ups. Sometimes, venture launches its product without knowing who will buy its products, for whom they are preparing the product. A critical consideration is how long will it take to determine who the customers are, as well as their buying habits. It is also important for the entrepreneur to understand what are new features looked by the consumer of their target market in the product they want to introduce and also check for its affordability from the market where the product is to be introduced.

2.8 Entrepreneurial Idea Generation

Entrepreneurial idea generation is the process of coming up with innovative concepts or solutions for new businesses, products, services, or ventures. Here are some key steps and methods often used in entrepreneurial idea generation:

- ***Identify Problems and Opportunities:*** Start by observing your surroundings, identifying pain points, inefficiencies, or unmet needs in the market. Look for gaps or areas where there is room for improvement or innovation.

- ***Market Research:*** Conduct thorough market research to understand current trends, consumer behavior, competition, and emerging opportunities. Analyze industry reports, customer feedback, and demographic data to identify potential niches or untapped markets.

- ***Brainstorming:*** Gather a diverse team or group of individuals and engage in brainstorming sessions to generate a wide range of ideas. Encourage creativity, open-mindedness, and free-flowing discussion without judgment. Use techniques like mind mapping, SWOT analysis, or SCAMPER to stimulate idea generation.

- ***Problem-Solving:*** Approach idea generation from a problem-solving perspective. Break down complex problems into smaller components and brainstorm solutions for each component. Look for innovative ways to address challenges or pain points in unique and effective ways.

- ***Customer-Centric Approach:*** Put yourself in the shoes of your target customers and empathize with their needs, preferences, and pain points. Use techniques like design thinking or customer journey mapping to gain insights into their experiences and identify opportunities for innovation.

- ***Prototype and Testing:*** Develop prototypes or minimum viable products (MVPs) to validate and test your ideas. Gather feedback from potential customers, stakeholders, or experts and iterate on your concepts based on their input. Use techniques like rapid prototyping or lean start-up methodologies to quickly iterate and refine your ideas.

- ***Networking and Collaboration:*** Engage with industry experts, mentors, or fellow entrepreneurs to share ideas, gain insights, and collaborate on new ventures. Attend networking events, workshops, or conferences to expand your network and access new opportunities for idea generation and development.

- ***Stay Curious and Keep Learning:*** Cultivate a mindset of curiosity, continuous learning, and exploration. Stay updated on industry trends, emerging technologies, and market dynamics. Be open to new ideas, perspectives, and sources of inspiration from diverse fields and disciplines.

- ***Evaluate and Prioritize:*** Once you have generated a list of ideas, evaluate each idea based on criteria such as feasibility, scalability, market potential, and alignment with your goals and values. Prioritize the most promising ideas and focus your resources and efforts on developing them further.

- ***Iterate and Refine:*** Idea generation is an iterative process, so be prepared to iterate, refine, and pivot as you gather feedback, test assumptions, and validate your concepts. Embrace failure as a learning opportunity and be willing to adapt and evolve your ideas based on new insights and experiences.

This is the first and most important stage in project identification. It is an intellectual process that requires vision, initiative, scheme and inquisitiveness. The Project idea can come out from one or more following sources:

- Trade fairs and trade journals.

- Through experience of others in the particular business,

- Success stories of friends, relatives.

- Surveys, reports, newspapers, periodicals.

- Detailed analysis of demand and supply

- Government policies and support for the development of the various sectors.

- Increasing demand of certain goods and services in the domestic market as well as foreign market.

- Easy Availability of raw material, skilled Labor

- Invention of new technology.

Idea can be generated with the help of the following methods:

a. Brainstorming: This technique was originally used by Alex Osborn in 1938 in an American company to persuade innovative thinking in a group of six to eight people. Through this method a large number of ideas are generated without any criticism. In this method, people are encouraged to produce as many ideas they can generate without any criticism and evaluation. It works on the principle of no criticism and quantity raises quality.

b. Focus Groups: This group consists of 6-12 members belonging to different socio-economic backgrounds to focus on the particular matter. The group has a moderator to have the detailed discussion. Ideas are generated and detailed discussions are carried on to identify the excellent ideas.

c. Problem Inventory analysis: This method is more like a focused group method but in this method along with generating ideas, it also considers the problem a product faces. In this method, focus group is provided with the list of the problems in a general product category and then identifying and discussing the problems of the products in that category.

Idea generation phase helps in opportunity scanning and opportunity identification and thus helps in identifying and idea and thus converting it into an opportunity. At the idea stage, there is a just an Idea of what to do but at the opportunity stage, entrepreneur actually converts his idea into opportunity by gaining insight into what actually to do. For e.g: Arjun and Raman are friends. Raman is working a company and Arjun is still searching for the job. Raman suggested Arjun to start a business, this is called an Idea. Later on after analyzing the various businesses, when Arjun has decided to go to start a transport business, then it is an opportunity. Therefore, this phase helps in identifying the opportunity.

Every successful idea for business must meet these three feasibility criteria.

Technical feasibility refers to the ability to develop and implement a business idea using the available technology. This includes factors such as the availability of materials, equipment, and skilled labor. For example, if you want to start a business that produces custom furniture, you will need to have access to the necessary tools and equipment, as well as skilled woodworkers.

Economic feasibility refers to the potential profitability of a business idea. This includes factors such as the cost of production, the price of the product or service, and the size of the target market. For example, if you want to start a business that sells organic dog food, you will need to determine the cost of ingredients, the price of competing products, and the number of potential customers in your area.

Market feasibility refers to the demand for a business idea. This includes factors such as the size of the target market, the level of competition, and the customer's willingness to pay for the product or service. For example, if you want to start a business that provides dog walking services, you will need to determine the number of potential customers in your area, the price of competing services, and the willingness of pet owners to pay for dog walking.

2.9 Identifying Business Opportunities

Are you an entrepreneur looking for the world best business opportunity? It's an exciting time to be in business - success stories from start-ups running the gamut from online fashion brands to ride-sharing app companies dominate the news and social media feeds.

But what does it take the identification of business opportunity, weigh its risks, knowing whether or not this is something that could work for you?

A business opportunity provides an individual or a company with an amazing chance to expand their current operations, initiate new offerings, and turn a profit. It can be found in any industry and often exists due to factors such as technology advancements, product development, market changes, skill gaps, and even financial benefits. Identification of entrepreneurial opportunities is an effective way to jumpstart your business endeavours.

The world best business opportunity offers advantages that include better access to resources, relatively easy entry into competitive markets, lower start-up costs, and the potential for significant profits. Whether you are a budding entrepreneur or an established business owner, exploring opportunities can open the door to increased success.

2.9.1 Importance of Business Opportunity

Business opportunities are essential for business growth and success. Having the right opportunities gives business owners, entrepreneurs, and investors the ability to maximize their potential and create a successful business enterprise. Identifying business opportunities can allow companies to increase their revenue streams by providing unique products, services, or an innovative approach to a problem.

Identification of business opportunities in entrepreneurship is an important step to kick-starting your career as an entrepreneur. There are numerous possibilities for entrepreneurs to explore, including harnessing technology or creating a new niche in an industry or sector, as well as identifying opportunities that involve taking advantage of changes in consumer behaviour or leveraging resources from other businesses. By correctly following well-defined steps in the identification of business opportunities, anyone has the potential to find success in entrepreneurship and create lucrative business ventures.

Having new business opportunities also provides access to increased capital resources, enabling businesses to invest in employee development, technology upgrades, and other growth strategies that can help propel business objectives. Therefore, paying close attention to available entrepreneurial opportunities is incredibly important for any business, regardless of size or industry.

2.10 Traits of a Good Business Opportunity

Let's explore the traits of the world best business opportunity. These traits are extremely useful if you are wondering along the lines of how to identify business opportunities.

- ***Clarity:*** Clarity is an essential trait of business opportunities, enabling entrepreneurs to make well-informed decisions. Having a clear understanding of business opportunities allows business owners to know exactly what they are getting and how the business will truly benefit them. Clear business opportunities provide reassurance that business owners can trust the opportunity, allowing them to confidently capitalize on it. Therefore, identifying business opportunities with crystal clear clarity on all aspects of entrepreneurship is important for your future success.

- ***Feasibility:*** Understanding the feasibility of business opportunities in India is an important trait when considering any business venture. For business owners, opportunities identification through this lens can provide vital feedback on what elements need to be addressed to make the business successful. By assessing all aspects of the business—including its financial impacts, longer-term goals, and timelines for completion—business owners can better understand how likely an opportunity is to bring positive returns.

- ***Relevance:*** Relevance is an essential factor to consider when you identify business opportunities and helps pick the ones that stand out from the rest. It ensures that business owners select business ideas that match industry trends and customer demand, which can help them acquire a larger customer base and generate more business profits. By remaining on top of trending topics, companies have a better chance of creating products and services in line with market demand and staying ahead of the competition.

- ***Scalability:*** Scalability is often the highly desirable trait for the world no 1 business opportunity. An opportunity can transition from small to large with minimal effort and increased benefit, allowing business owners to increase the returns from investments without having to dedicate more resources or effort. For business owners looking to identify opportunities that can quickly and efficiently generate growth, scalability must be carefully considered and evaluated before investing in a business.

- ***Profitability:*** Profitability is certainly one of the most important traits of business opportunities identification; it indicates that the business is successful and capable of providing its owners with legitimate returns. Consistent profitability serves as an indication of long-term sustainability and can be used as a measuring stick for business growth over time.

2.10.1 Types of Business Opportunity

Let's explore some of the common types of business opportunities.

- ***New Market Opportunity:*** New Market Opportunity is a specific type of business opportunity that focuses on growing an existing business into a new and untapped market. They are attracted to companies that seek the potential for rapid growth but can be risky because the risks may be in markets where the business is unfamiliar. Companies looking to take advantage of new market opportunities need to understand the market conditions, do their due diligence on needs and regulations, and make sure expectations are realistic.

- ***Distributorship:*** For business owners looking to generate business growth, a distributorship business opportunity can prove to be an invaluable asset. Distributors sell products for manufacturers, thus giving them access to a wider customer base with less effort. There are no entry barriers when joining a distributorship business, so this business opportunity is perfect for those hoping to make their mark on the business world with minimal investment. Furthermore, by collaborating with professionals in their field, business owners have the potential to learn and grow their skill sets while also growing their businesses.

- ***Competitive Opportunity:*** Competitive opportunity is one such business opportunity that stands out. It allows business owners to secure more business and stay ahead of the competition. This business opportunity offers a better return on investment through strategic planning, dynamic marketing strategies, and leveraging technology and data to drive growth efficiently.

- ***Franchising:*** Franchising is a business opportunity that provides an innovative way to start and expand a business. It allows an individual or business to leverage the proven business model of another company and grow their business quickly while typically involving fewer risks. This business opportunity supports the development of new business models, bringing more flexible options to entrepreneurs who are just starting or established business owners looking to diversify their brands.

- ***Technology Opportunity:*** Technology opportunity is a great business prospect for those interested in staying abreast of today's cutting-edge developments. Rather than relying solely on traditional business models, savvy entrepreneurs are turning to these new tools and services that can provide the means to bridge the gap between their business goals and the technology solutions necessary to achieve them. As a business opportunity, technological solutions offer sizable returns due to their flexible deployment, cost efficiency, and ability to tailor solutions specifically designed for each enterprise's needs.

- ***Marketing:*** Marketing is an ever-evolving business opportunity that should be given serious consideration by prospective business owners. By using techniques to understand customer needs, create interesting and effective campaigns, and measure the success of those campaigns, business owners have the potential to dramatically increase the profit margins of their clients while also creating a positive brand identity and strong customer base.

- ***Licensing:*** Licensing is a business opportunity that offers the perfect balance of autonomy and support. Through licensing agreements, business owners join forces with existing business entities to share branding, resources, and customer bases. This offers the chance to benefit from the existing strength of a business without having to build up your market presence from scratch.

- ***Niche Opportunity:*** By honing in on a particular market or demographic, you can identify needs that would not be apparent in heavily saturated business arenas. Focusing on niche markets allows for the development of customized approaches to business success with greater precision and accuracy than the traditional business model.

2.11 Identify Business Opportunity

Whether its new business opportunities or entrepreneurial opportunities, there are many ways to identify business opportunities. Let's take a look:

2.11.1 Steps in Identification of Business Opportunities

Here are some of the steps in identification of business opportunities:

1. Conduct market research to identify industry trends, customer needs, and potential gaps in the market.

2. Analyze the competition to understand their strengths and weaknesses.

3. Identify potential target markets and customer segments.

4. Evaluate the feasibility of the opportunity, including a financial analysis of the potential revenue and expenses.

5. Develop a business plan outlining the strategy for pursuing the opportunity.

6. Test and validate the opportunity through market research and pilot projects.

7. Take the necessary steps to capitalize on the opportunity, like acquiring funding or assembling a team.

2.11.2 Methods of Identifying Business Opportunities

There are many business opportunities in India, given the diverse market and demographics. But how can you identify the business opportunity suitable for you? Here are some ways how to identify business opportunities.

2.11.2.1 Environment Scanning

Environmental scanning involves monitoring external factors like economic, political, and technological trends that can impact a business. It helps to identify opportunities and threats that may affect the business in the future. Keeping a close watch on the changing Environment can facilitate business expansion or explore new business opportunities.

2.11.2.2 SWOT Analysis

SWOT analysis is a strategic planning tool to helps businesses identifies their strengths, weaknesses, opportunities, and threats. It helps in identifying internal and external factors that can impact the business and can be used to develop a plan of action.

2.11.2.3 Innovation Brainstorming

Innovation involves continuously exploring new technologies, processes, or business models to find new ways to create value for customers. With innovative brainstorming, new ideas and possibilities for products, services, or business models could be discovered by gathering a group of people to brainstorm. It can help identify new opportunities for growth and expansion- like online business opportunities for your current business or automating certain aspects of it like inventory planning.

2.11.2.4 Market Research

Market research involves analyzing data on consumer preferences, market trends, and industry statistics to identify potential areas for growth or untapped markets. Conducting market research will enable you to identify entrepreneurial business opportunities to come with products or services your customers are looking for.

2.11.2.5 Social Listening & Monitoring

Social listening and monitoring entail observing or monitoring social media and other online platforms to stay informed about industry trends, customer preferences, and competitors' activities. It can help identify the best business opportunities in India for reaching new customers or improving products and services.

2.11.3 Factors to Consider While Identifying Business Opportunities

Are you seeking the world no 1 business opportunity like every aspiring entrepreneur out there? Here are some factors to consider to identify the business opportunity suitable for you:

- ***Availability of Raw Materials:*** This ensures you have the necessary resources, such as materials, equipment, and labor, to produce a product or provide a service. Raw materials are essential for any business opportunity to manifest into a functional one.

- ***Internal Demand Analysis:*** Internal demand analysis analyses the potential demand for a product or service within the company or organization. This can lead to business expansion and identify opportunities within your current business. Who knows, you could even end up starting an online business for a new business dimension altogether.

- ***Market Size:*** Market size helps to determine the potential demand for a product or service in the broader market. Knowing the market size for a particular product or service can help determine the potential demand and growth and lead to the identification of business opportunity.

- ***Management Skillsets:*** Management skills are crucial for world no 1 business opportunity to manifest into a successful venture. The skills and experience of the management team are necessary for your business to run.

- ***Access to the customers:*** The ability to reach and sell to the target market for a particular product or service is important for your business opportunities to flourish. You need to have the right marketing strategy to reach your customers and ensure they have access to the service or products you are providing. (Here are some good customer acquisition strategies for your reference.)

- ***Need for Financing:*** Most importantly, ensure the financial resources required to start and run the business, including funding for initial start-up costs, ongoing expenses, order management, and future growth.

- ***Passion:*** An entrepreneur's enthusiasm and drive for the business opportunity drive the business forward. Likewise, a passion for the business can sustain motivation and effort through the challenges of starting and growing a business.

2.11.4 Objectives of Identifying Business Opportunity

You may wonder why you should put effort and energy into identification of business opportunity. Here are some objectives behind discovering business opportunities:

2.11.4.1 Types of Small Business Opportunity

Taking a chance with business opportunities is not easy for everyone and the fear of not succeeding stops many. You don't have to start big. Here are some small business opportunities to explore:

- ***Service-based businesses:*** The service sector is on the rise. Why not try your luck with it? You could offer consulting, accounting, or cleaning services to your consumers based on your interest.

- ***Retail Business:*** If you like managing a store and selling products, try retail business. Retail business opportunities enable you to sell the products to customers. It could be anything from a beauty store, clothing, stationery or grocery store.

- ***Online Businesses:*** There are also many online business opportunities like tutoring, digital marketing, e-commerce (be it B2B ecommerce or B2C), web designing, e-learning, etc.

- ***Home-bases Business:*** You could even explore new business opportunities from home. For instance, day care, e-commerce store, chocolate making, baking, handmade products, etc.

- ***Mobile Business:*** These businesses operate primarily out of vehicles, such as food trucks or hair salons. (Register with Amazon Business to explore the supplies for your mobile business.)

- ***Social Enterprise:*** Ever thought of establishing a social enterprise? You could develop business strategies to achieve social or environmental goals, like starting an NGO or cause-based organization.

- ***Niche Market Business:*** People are becoming more conscious and looking for specific products to sustain their lifestyles or choices. And niche businesses focus on a specific market or customer segment, such as organic food, eco-friendly products or pet grooming.

- ***Dropshipping Business:*** A popular business model in the e-commerce industry. Droshipping business saves you the hassle of inventory planning and management. You have to find the right suppliers with quality products to ensure the right product reaches your consumers.

- ***Online Education or e-learning Business:*** The e-learning sector is booming and online education is helping learners across. If you have the skills and subject expertise, why not offer customers online courses, webinars, or other educational content?

2.11.4.2 Types of Online Business Opportunity

Identification of entrepreneurial opportunities to test your luck is easier in the digital era. We have listed some of the online business opportunities from home or otherwise for you to consider:

- ***E-commerce:*** It is a tested business to explore. Selling products online is easier than you think. With a descriptive website and quality products, tapping into the online market is possible.

- ***Digital Marketing:*** If you have got a knack for marketing, with digital marketing, you could help companies or business to promote their products or services online through various channels such as SEO, PPC, social media marketing, and email marketing.

- ***Content Creation:*** Content creation has a vast scope. Put your love for writing to good use and create digital content like blogs, videos, podcasts, or e-books for businesses.

- ***Online Education/ e-learning:*** E-learning is a vastly growing sector. Working professionals, students, housewives, and people resuming from career breaks are looking for a convenient way to learn and that's where online education takes precedence.

- ***Consulting or Coaching:*** You could also offer consulting and expert advice to clients via online platforms. Being a life coach is also another option to explore. This is also one of the online business opportunities from home to consider.

- ***Affiliate Marketing:*** Affiliate marketing enables you to promote products and services from other companies or businesses and earn a commission for each sale. You could also use social media influences to push the products and gain commission.

- ***Offer Online Services:*** You could also start an online service business and deploy skills like graphic design, video editing, photography, web designing & development, virtual assistance, etc.

- ***Online Marketplace:*** Why not help businesses and create a platform or online marketplace for the buyers and sellers to conduct business? Amazon Business or Amazon is doing just that.

- ***Online Survey or Research:*** Business, organization, or companies needs to study the market, product reception, consumer behavior, and more to find new avenues to grow and understand where they lack. With an online survey or research business, you could provide the data and information for businesses or organizations.

- ***Online Gaming:*** A very popular business option to explore. There is a community of online gamers out there and you would be helping them with their favortie activity by starting an online gaming platform. One of the fun online business opportunities from home as well for gamers.

- ***Dropshipping:*** Dropshipping is yet another business venture to consider for online business opportunities. Be the front man offering the goods to your consumer without the tension of managing the inventory.

2.11.4.3 Types of Business Opportunities from Home

Identification of entrepreneurial opportunities is also possible for home-based businesses. You can run and manage a business from the comfort of your home. Here's a list of business opportunities to consider if you like work from home set up:

- ***Freelancing:*** You could try freelancing from home. Based on the skill or skills you have to offer, like content writing, teaching, video editing, graphics designing, etc. If you want flexibility, then freelancing is the way to go.

- ***Consultancy:*** Put your knowledge and experience to good use and start a consulting firm. Help companies or organizations with their problems. Make a list of your skills and experience and decide how that could be utilized in the market.

- ***Art and Crafts Teaching:*** Love teaching and have a knack for creativity? Try teaching art and crafts. DIY is in trend and people want to create things themselves, help them create handmade items and feel fulfilled.

- ***Graphics Designing:*** Many businesses, micro or large, rely on graphic designers for their logos, posters, newsletters, etc. Thus, graphic designing is a great online business opportunity to consider. If you got the skills and the equipment, go for it.

- ***Home-based food business:*** If you enjoy cooking or baking, there are several home-based food businesses to consider. You could start a bakery, tiffin service, homey restaurant, etc., cook your heart out, and make some money.

- ***Coaching or tutoring:*** You could also try coaching or tutoring from the comfort of your home. You just need to decide your target audience, kind of service offered (one-on-one or group), decide on rates, and market your business well.

- ***Blogging:*** Blogging is an old and tested work from home business opportunity if you enjoy writing. Many companies and businesses use blogs to generate traffic and create potential leads, and you could help them do that with the right skills.

- ***Nutritionist or Health Guide:*** Everyone cares about their health, but some need guidance to realign their eating habits, nutrition intake, and maintain and healthy lifestyle. Being a health guide and nutritionist will come in handy for them.

- ***Event Planning:*** Event planning is another fun business opportunity if you like planning events. Find the right clients and do an impeccable job on your first project and your portfolio will write itself.

- ***Starting YouTube Channel:*** You could start a YouTube channel and follow your passion. It could be anything from a cooking channel to teaching, DIY, hacks, etc.

2.12 Managing Skill for Value Creation

Managing Skills for Value Creation are essential capabilities that entrepreneurs and business leaders need to effectively generate and deliver value to customers, stakeholders, and society. These skills encompass strategic planning, resource allocation, decision-making, and leadership, all aimed at maximizing the long-term impact and sustainability of a business. By mastering these skills, entrepreneurs can identify opportunities, optimize processes, and drive innovation, ultimately creating a competitive advantage and fostering growth in an ever-evolving marketplace. Effective management for value creation is central to turning ideas into profitable and sustainable business ventures.

2.12.1 Value Creation in Business

Value creation identifies the intersection between the overlapping interests of customers, stakeholders, and the organization itself. A successful business model leverages all of these values within company initiatives.

Value creation is offering products that meet and exceed customers' expectations. When a company inspires customer loyalty, profits increase. When stakeholders receive high returns on their investments, they're willing to contribute more capital. This capital sustains the company's future initiatives, such as increased employee benefits and training. When employees are valued, productivity and product innovation increase.

2.12.2 Importance of value creation

Investing in value creation sparks a cycle of sustained advantages for all aspects of your business. In other words, the value creation trade-offs keep your business profitable so you can continue doing what you're doing – and do it even better. These are the key areas influenced by value creation:

- ***Sustainable business success:*** Targeted value creation ensures long-term value for this quarter and for years to come. Without a clear vision of the company's objectives, initiatives are unfocused. When resources aren't sustainably allocated, cash flow halts, the bottom line decreases, and future endeavors are at a disadvantage.

- ***Customer satisfaction:*** The customer relationship doesn't end at the buying decision. In fact, it begins with the creation of value. Sustained customer satisfaction results in continued business with supportive consumers. These long-term customers inspire new purchases through word-of-mouth product recommendations to their friends and family.

- ***Competitive advantage:*** When value creation informs your company's initiatives, it keeps your offerings top-of-mind and your name at the top of the food chain. The shutdown of many businesses during the COVID-19 pandemic proves that having a competitive advantage does more than increase profits – it can keep your company alive during times of strained financial returns.

- ***Stakeholder engagement:*** Within a company's practices, value creation can take the form of transparent communication regarding goals, performance, and assets with stakeholders. This clarity sustains the balance between internal initiatives and stakeholder engagement. The decision-making process strengthens when these perspectives align.

- ***Financial performance:*** Understanding the values and needs of customers, stakeholders, and the organization results in the most competitive pricing that both appeals to customers and optimizes profits. When the creation of value takes center stage in the decision-making process, financial returns are fully realized because of the precision of company initiatives.

- ***Innovation and adaptability:*** Change is the only constant, and customer needs are no exception. Without refocusing efforts and innovating your offerings, your customers will find another company that can meet their evolving expectations.

2.13 Creating and Sustaining Enterprising Model

Research on "sustainable business models" (SBM) and "business models for sustainability" (BMfS) is gaining momentum and shows first traits of a field in its own right (Lüdeke-Freund & Dembek, 2017). An important questions in this area is:

How to define a "sustainable business model" or "business model for sustainability"?*

Such a definition would be an important ingredient for further conceptual and theoretical work.

Below you find a list of definitions that emerged and evolved in our research over the last ten years. They take different theoretical starting points (such as re-defining customer value or connecting to the business case for sustainability) and emphasise different business model functions (such as creating competitive advantage or supporting different kinds of innovation).

This list is neither complete nor does it provide final or ultimate definitions. It should rather be seen as a collection of snapshots of an ongoing research process and an impulse for your own work in this field.

2.13.1 What does a Sustainable Business Model Mean?

Something that is sustainable is something that will last beyond the present at the same level or rate it is at now. Otherwise put, it is something that meets needs in the present without compromising the needs of the future.

It follows, then, that a sustainable business model is one that generates revenue now without draining resources for business and development in the future. A good sustainable business model will recognise and value the economic, social and environmental values of all stakeholders.

It is important to make a distinction here between a business model that is sustainable, and one that focuses on sustainability. Although a strong sustainable business model must take into account environmental sustainability, it doesn't necessarily focus on it. However, with eco-friendly trends becoming clearer and stronger, having a sustainability focus can add to the strength of an already-strong business model.

A good sustainable business model will have:

- A plan on how to stay financially viable (economic focus)

- A plan for staying relevant and successful in a future with volatile energy sources and rising commodity prices (environmental focus)

- A plan to engage in society and capture the ethos of the public (social focus)

2.13.2 What is a sustainable strategy?

A sustainable strategy aims to unite economic, social, and environmental goals in order to create consistent business and revenue. Utilising these three areas will strengthen the identity of the business and create a touchstone for future endeavours. Creating a strategy around these three areas will help you to understand the flow of business as well: both money that comes in and goes out, as well as resources that are being used and created.

The strategy itself will assist the business in taking steps towards becoming sustainable and maintaining that sustainability in the long run. A truly sustainable strategy should be sufficient to see the business through at least 20 years of development before it needs updating.

Being strategic is not going to be quick or particularly easy. You will need to know the trends and long-term predictions relating to your industry. You will need a comprehensive knowledge of your customer base and target market. You will also need an intricate and nuanced understanding of your own brand and business values and goals.

Start with a purpose or values statement and answer the most vital questions your business needs to ask to develop a strategy:

- Why does this business exist?

- What solutions does this business offer and what problems does it aim to address?

- How does this business improve society, the economy, and the environment?

Knowing how to answer all of these questions will help you to create a brand identity. Your brand identity will then inform all further decisions around modelling and strategizing for the future.

With an identity in place, it's time to start planning out a sustainable strategy. A good sustainable strategy should include:

- *The strategic context:* all global and local sustainability issues that impact your business now or could impact it in the future. Focusing on, and prioritising, contextual sustainability goals.

- *The vision:* the long-range goals, aspirations, and plans for the business. Without vision, strategy has no end point, but with no strategy, vision is just a dream. Carefully lay out the vision of the business in the context of the environmental, social, and economic landscape.

- ***Action point:*** all the steps you plan to take to follow the strategy and achieve the vision. A full implementation plan will make the strategy easier to follow and will give clear steps. This is especially important when a business hits rough times because having a strategy that is well-researched and carefully planned gives you something to clearly guide you through difficulties.

- ***Timescales:*** a clear idea of when each step should take place. Predicted trends will factor into the timescale, as will predicted growth and business development. Have an idea of when each step should take place and how long it should take to help you stay on track and stay strategic.

- ***Reporting:*** a recording and reporting plan for your strategy. To help you stay focused, make sure there are measures in place to keep you accountable to your strategy. How will you record progress" Who will be reviewing the records and reports" How will you stay accountable to your own sustainable strategy?

2.13.3 Creating a Sustainable Business Model

Build sustainability into the ethos of your business to tap into the over 50% of people who are changing their lives to become more environmentally friendly. There are simple steps that you can take in creating your business model that will allow you to compete for longer in this demanding sustainability shift.

- ***Start with values:*** You can change a lot about your business, but you can't change the core values once your business has grown – at least not without a lot of difficulty. By building sustainability into the core beliefs and values of your business, you create a stronger starting point that will be able to support future development.

- ***Shape values into something valuable:*** Your values cannot support your business on your own. The next step is to think about how your values will make your goods or services more valuable. A fashion business, for instance, cannot rely on simply having a sustainable value, the products still need to be fashionable. But when fashion and sustainability are working together, it increases the value of the product, making your business more attractive.

- **_Be future focused:_** The assumption is that businesses will grow. When you are planning your business growth, consider how increased workforce, the need for larger premises, higher energy consumption, and geographical expansion might influence your sustainability. As your business grows, it will draw more on natural resources. Your job now is to consider how you can lighten that burden by planning for sustainability in the future.

- **_Think about your resources:_** Every business uses resources. Are the resources your business uses sustainable Where do they come from and how are they replenished Are your supplies environmentally friendly from source or are you only looking at them from the middle of production onwards" It is your responsibility to know where your resources come from to ensure sustainability.

- **_Be generous:_** Stakeholders often place more long-term trust in businesses that have shown they value sustainability in tangible ways. This long-term trust is vital to your long-term growth. Find ways to give back to the community – volunteering, donating, going green, and joining sustainability initiatives are all good ways of giving back to the environment and the community that you want to support you.

- **_Think sustainably:_** Consider ways in which your office or storefront could be more sustainable. It may be as simple as having more recycling options or changing to more energy-efficient light-bulbs. Or you could end up "greening" the whole building and switching to fully sustainable energy sources. Whichever it is, make sure that sustainability is constantly on your radar.

- ***Promote sustainability:*** Finally, get your stakeholders, employees, and colleagues on board with your sustainability plans. The more support you have, the easier it will be to create corporate structures that support a sustainable business model.

2.13.4 Five Elements for a Sustainable Business Model

Based in systems theory, approaching sustainability as resilience reveals some important insights into organizational forms, some of which I describe below.

- ***Diversity:*** The firm needs a diverse set of resources, people and investments to be resilient. While diverse investments are seen to draw on resources and absorb managerial attention, a single line of business, single sources of revenues, or people with similar mindsets can expose the firm to greater risks. Firms can no longer simply 'stick to the knitting.'

- ***Modularity:*** Matrixed organizations are often seen as facilitating knowledge flows. However, such organizations are not only resource intensive, they expose the whole organization to shocks as they reverberate through the organization. Organizations need to be less interdependent, and focus on modularity (keeping functions separate), so they can be insulated from shocks.

- ***Openness:*** Resilient firms must know what's going on outside their boundaries. These firms can sense issues on the horizon. They are constantly monitoring the external environment, and drawing scenarios of possible futures. They expect not only to react to those potential futures, but also help to shape them. The link between the organization and the external business and natural environment is vital, permeable, and malleable.

- ***Slack resources:*** In an era of just-in-time production, slack or spare resources are often seen as costly and wasteful. However, innovation and adaptation requires both financial and creative investments, and the space to change direction. Firms that can ride storms must allow for a little more time to accommodate new ideas, scenarios, and shifts in thinking. Slack resources, both assets and capabilities, are always considered as very important to shape a sustainable business model.

- ***Matching cycles:*** Firms often think about optimizing performance and getting more from less. But, this thinking puts firms on a treadmill, doing the same thing faster every day—and, it has them bumping up against resource constraints. Resilient businesses think, not about constant growth, but rather about cyclical processes: cycles of growth and contraction, cycles of production, and cycles of consumer purchase patterns.

2.13.5 Examples of Sustainable Business Models

With plenty of business sustainability models available (including the doughnut economics model we covered in another blog), it's important for companies to assess which ones relate closest to their product, service and goals. Here are three popular examples:

1. The eight-step sustainable business model by Szekely and Dossa

The Francisco Szekely and Zahir Dossa eight-step model approaches sustainability beyond the triple-bottom-line by exploring steps ranging from organisational purpose to PR transparency. They propose that businesses should focus on addressing a societal need from the get-go and view profitability as not an end point, but a method of supporting sustainability. Here are their eight steps to success:

- ***Sustainability mission:*** What is the purpose of your organisation?

- ***Long-term vision:*** What will your organisation look like in twenty-five years?

- ***Sustainability strategy:*** Identify your stakeholders and develop a plan to impact them in a positive way.

- ***Implementing sustainability strategy:*** How can you engage your stakeholders for maximum impact?

- ***Measuring sustainability performance:*** How do you measure non-financial performance?

- ***Transparency and accountability:*** Can you pass the newspaper test?

- ***Scaling:*** Can sustainability scale?

- ***Sustainability innovation:*** What makes sustainability innovations unique?

2. The eight sustainable business model archetypes by Bocken, Short and Evans

The eight sustainable business model archetypes from Nancy Bocken, Sam Short and Steve Evans describe the solutions and opportunities that organisations can take advantage of when building a business model for sustainability. The eight tactics were developed to accelerate the research and practice of sustainable business models:

- Maximise material and energy efficiency.

- Create value from 'waste'.

- Substitute with renewables and natural processes.

- Deliver functionality rather than ownership.

- Adopt a stewardship role.

- Encourage sufficiency.

- Re-purpose the business for society/environment.

- Develop scale-up solutions.

3. The triple layered business model canvas (TLBMC) by Joyce and Paquin

Alexandre Joyce and Raymond Paquin designed the triple layered business model canvas (TLBMC) to explore methods of sustainable innovation in business.

The TLBMC is a tool for integrating environmental and social factors into an organisations business model through a lifecycle approach and stakeholder perspective. The addition of the environmental and social layers to the economic layer of the business model canvas can generate multiple types of value.

- ***Economic:*** Considering partners, activities, resources, value proposition, customer relationships, channels and customer segments.

- ***Environmental:*** Considering supplies and outsourcing, production, materials, functional value, end-of-life use, distribution and user phase.

- ***Social:*** Considering local communities, governance, employees, social value, societal culture, scale of outreach and the end user.

2.13.6 Businesses Implement Sustainable Business Models

To effectively build sustainability into a business's DNA and overcome sustainability issues, here are some possible steps to follow:

- Evaluate current practices to understand areas for improvement.

- Engage stakeholders at all levels and listen to their opinions to build support.

- Identify a sustainable business model which closely aligns to your needs.

- Set measurable objectives to achieve long-term sustainability goals.

- Innovate your purpose, product and processes using your elected sustainable business model as a framework.

- Communicate developments in your sustainability efforts transparently and consistently to relevant business stakeholders and customers.

- Monitor your business's progress against key performance indicators and continually seek out improvements.

2.14 Organizational Effectiveness

An effective organization is a company that successfully meets its goals. These goals may be external, such as producing a certain quality product, or internal, such as improving communication within a company. An effective organization examines various factors in a company, like how well employees perform to the efficiency of a business process, and seeks opportunities to improve. For instance, if an organization defined its goal as reaching a 10% increase in subscribers, it could determine its effectiveness by looking at how many more subscribers it got in a set period.

2.14.1 Benefits of Organizational Effectiveness

Organizational effectiveness is important in helping companies flourish long term. It allows organizations to operate more smoothly by keeping them focused on their goals. Benefits of an effective organization include:

- ***Increased productivity:*** Setting clear goals and monitoring progress may increase output.

- ***Strengthened employee engagement:*** Employees who know their goals and why they're important may connect more with their work.

- ***Enhanced management communication:*** Taking steps toward organizational effectiveness can help managers align.

- ***Optimized budget:*** Organizational effectiveness typically helps you eliminate areas of waste.

- ***Streamlined use of technology:*** A company may upgrade or improve its equipment by promoting efficiency.

- ***Maximized customer value:*** More effective organizations may be more capable of meeting customers' needs.

- ***Related:*** Careers in Organizational Development

2.14.2 Types of organizational effectiveness models

An organization's effectiveness depends on what goal it set out to achieve. Several models help companies determine their effectiveness based on their key objectives. Here are some organizational effectiveness models businesses use:

1. Internal process model: In the internal process model, companies focus on internal processes and protocols to make the organization function. By optimizing processes, these companies may improve their operations and increase their productivity. Ways organizations can achieve this include having a thorough process for documentation and suitable equipment to enable functions.

2. Goal model: A goal model focuses on accomplishing an organization's objectives. This is a traditional model used to measure an organization's effectiveness. An organization may set various goals, ranging from reaching a financial target to creating a particular societal impact. The goal model might be less actionable than other models, as it focuses on measuring outputs and has little information about the inputs or processes.

3. Resource-based model: Organizations using a resource-based model measure their effectiveness by looking at their inputs. This approach focuses on the idea that companies can become successful by obtaining an adequate supply of the resources required to perform well. To do this, organizations try to mine rare, valuable and unique resources to create a competitive advantage over other organizations. For example, a social media company may own proprietary software that is challenging to copy.

4. Strategic constituency model: A strategic constituency model is one in which companies evaluate their success by measuring their ability to meet the needs of their environment. Companies that use this approach aim to rise to the standards of parties that control their success. These constituencies can include business owners, employees, customers, suppliers or the government, as each of these groups can influence the organization's survival. To be successful in this approach, businesses identify their constituencies and their expectations so that they can fulfill them.

5. Abundance model: An abundance model measures an organization's effectiveness by examining its positive impact on humankind. To companies using this approach, effectiveness means prioritizing appropriate beliefs to maximize human capabilities. Abundance models use a combination of positive and negative values to embrace the full scope of human potential.

6. Competing values model: In a competing values model, organizations determine their effectiveness by their ability to create competing values. This approach focuses on different key values like Cameron and Quinn's competing values framework. For example, a company might aim to collaborate freely while competing in the marketplace and promoting a healthy work environment. This approach encourages teams to focus on all three goals to build a productive team.

2.14.3 Improve Organizational Effectiveness

Follow these steps to maximize a company's organizational effectiveness:

1. Set a goal: In create an effective organization, first, identify what area of the business you want to improve. This allows you to set clear objectives to achieve. An example of a goal for a company might be improving the customer experience. Once you set your goal, ensure all team members are aware of it so they can work to help achieve it.

2. Make effective decisions: Since decision-making is a key component of organizational effectiveness, it's important for professionals at all levels in a company to make the right choices. When making decisions, ensure they align with the organization's goals and values. Create an effective communication system that allows you to share decisions with your team members and gather input. In the example of an organization wanting to improve their customer experience, this might involve collectively brainstorming ways to enhance a customer's experience with their company.

3. Develop strategies: Strategy can help a team build an actionable plan to achieve goals. Evaluate where the organization currently is and what obstacles it can overcome to improve its position. It might be worthwhile to study other organizations to learn what strategies worked for them. For instance, a company looking to improve its customer experience may implement a rewards program for loyal customers to encourage brand loyalty and engage with customers authentically on social media to establish a digital community.

4. Consider your needs: At this stage in your effective organizational planning, you can identify what resources the organization requires to meet its objectives. Determine what type of employees might help the company fulfill the strategies. For example, if you want to track customer satisfaction data more effectively, it might be important to hire an experienced data analyst on the customer satisfaction team. The team can then hire the right people and train existing employees to fill skill gaps.

5. Measure your effectiveness: Finally, assess how successful the company was at reaching its objectives. One way to measure your effectiveness is using a scorecard to determine if the organization met its goals or key performance indicators (KPIs). Regularly track your progress to identify areas for improvement and see what went well. Using the previous example, the company may notice that hiring a data analyst helped provide them with meaningful insights and helped create more loyal consumers.

2.14.1 Types of Metrics to Measure Business Success

Here are some ideas that can be important to leaders when they're trying to improve organizational effectiveness:

Metrics: It's important to measure the right figures to evaluate your progress. Setting concrete goals and using numerical data to track organizational effectiveness can be beneficial. Qualitative data is also important, but quantitative data encourages transparency and accountability. Define the best KPIs for each team to track.

Company culture: A positive work environment might motivate employees, promote collaboration and increase productivity. It may be helpful for managers to describe the current company culture in their workplace and brainstorm small ways they can improve engagement and promote organizational values. For example, if the company values risk-taking, you might decide to host a company outing where you perform fun, safe challenges to encourage employees to embrace risks.

People: Knowing what people can make an organization effective can improve hiring and help you promote the right people to leadership positions. Think about the values, skills and character traits that make a productive member of your team. Each department may have its own unique answers, but they must align to create a collaborative and effective workforce.

Priorities: Collaborate with your colleagues to determine what's important to the organization. Rank your objectives to determine where you plan to dedicate most of the team's energy, time and resources. Priorities can shift as business needs change, so it might be beneficial to revisit this conversation periodically.

2.14.5 Creating Organizational Effectiveness

You can use this advice to help you create organizational effectiveness in the workplace:

- ***Ask for feedback.*** For an organization to continue to improve and become more effective, it's helpful to be open to suggestions and feedback from others.

- ***Train new hires well.*** Since people play an essential role in organizational effectiveness, it's important to consider how new employees can contribute to a company's goals.

- ***Find the right tools.*** To maximize organizational effectiveness, be open to using tools, such as technology, to improve the workflow.

2.14.6 Factors Impacting Organizational Effectiveness

Strategic Human Resource Consultant, Corporate Trainer, Entrepreneur, Influencer, Certified DISC Practitioner, MBA Faculty, Editorial Board Member, Advisory Board Member, Coach

Organizational effectiveness refers to the extent to which an organization achieves its goals and objectives while utilizing its resources efficiently. It is a measure of how well an organization performs and delivers value to its stakeholders. Here are some key factors that contribute to organizational effectiveness:

1. Clear Vision, Mission, and Goals: An effective organization has a well-defined vision, mission, and goals that provide a sense of direction and purpose. These statements outline the organization's aspirations, values, and the outcomes it aims to achieve. They serve as guiding principles for decision-making, strategy formulation, and resource allocation.

2. Strong Leadership: Leadership plays a crucial role in driving organizational effectiveness. Effective leaders inspire and motivate employees, provide clear guidance, and make strategic decisions that align with the organization's objectives. They create a positive work culture, foster innovation, and empower employees to perform at their best.

3. Strategic Planning: A well-developed strategic plan helps organizations align their resources, capabilities, and actions to achieve their goals. It involves analyzing the internal and external environment, setting priorities, and formulating strategies to address challenges and leverage opportunities. Effective strategic planning ensures that the organization is focused, adaptable, and responsive to changes in the business landscape.

4. Efficient Resource Management: Organizational effectiveness relies on the efficient management of resources, including human resources, financial capital, technology, and infrastructure. Effective organizations allocate resources strategically, optimize processes, and continuously monitor and evaluate resource utilization to maximize productivity and minimize waste.

5. Clear Communication: Effective communication is essential for organizational effectiveness. It ensures that information flows smoothly across all levels and functions of the organization. Clear communication helps align employees' efforts, disseminate goals and objectives, facilitate collaboration, and foster a culture of transparency and accountability.

6. Talent Management: Organizations that effectively attract, develop, and retain talent tend to be more successful. Effective talent management involves recruiting the right people, providing training and development opportunities, promoting a culture of continuous learning, and recognizing and rewarding performance. By nurturing a skilled and motivated workforce, organizations can enhance their overall effectiveness.

2.14.7 Performance Measurement and Continuous Improvement

Effective organizations establish performance metrics and regularly measure progress towards their goals. They have mechanisms in place to monitor key performance indicators (KPIs) and evaluate outcomes. This data-driven approach allows them to identify areas for improvement, make informed decisions, and continuously enhance their processes and performance.

Adaptability and Change Management: Organizational effectiveness requires the ability to adapt to changing market conditions, customer needs, and technological advancements. Effective organizations embrace innovation, encourage creativity, and proactively manage change. They are agile and responsive, constantly seeking ways to improve and stay ahead of the competition.

Stakeholder Engagement: Engaging with stakeholders, including customers, employees, suppliers, and the community, is crucial for organizational effectiveness. Effective organizations listen to their stakeholders' needs and expectations, seek feedback, and build strong relationships. By understanding and meeting stakeholder demands, organizations can enhance their reputation, customer loyalty, and overall performance.

2.14.8 Differences between Organizational Effectiveness and Efficiency

To be effective is a different practice from being efficient. They look like they should mean the same thing but they do not.

Effectiveness is how well your team can follow work procedures to achieve set goals. When you aim for something and you get it precisely right, what you did was effective.

Efficiency is how well your employees can accomplish tasks without wasting time, effort and resources—how you can use fewer resources, less time and less money to achieve the same goal.

You become more efficient when you reach your targets effectively and more quickly. Efficiency requires effectiveness.

You set a goal to produce and deliver a certain amount of goods to customers. You hit that goal three weeks after you set it. The processes and strategies you followed to achieve that goal were effective. Now, if you're able to produce and deliver that same number of goods in two weeks without expending more resources, you've become more efficient.

2.14.9 Approaches of Evaluating Organizational Effectiveness

There are also several different approaches to evaluate your organization's effectiveness.

2.14.9.1 External Approach

The external approach evaluates the organization's ability to secure, manage and control scarce and valued skills and resources such as skilled personnel, capital and raw materials.

Set effectiveness goals by doing the following:

- Obtain high-quality input of raw materials and employees.

- Increase market share.

- Increase stock price.

- Gain the support of stakeholders.

2.14.9.2 Internal Approach

The internal approach evaluates the organization's ability to be innovative and function quickly. It focuses on minimizing strain, integrating individuals and the organization, and conducting smooth and efficient operations. In this approach, effectiveness is the capability to get better at internal efficiency, coordination, commitment and staff satisfaction. Other aspects such as resources, outputs and satisfaction of clientele or participants are ignored. There is a clear linkage between the internal processes such as decision making and staffing and desired outputs.

To be effective, you should:

- Cut decision-making time.

- Increase the rate of product innovation.

- Increase coordination and motivation of the employee.

- Reduce conflict.

- Reduce time to the market.

2.14.9.3 Technological Approach

The technological approach evaluates the organization's ability to convert skills and resources into goods and services.

To achieve effectiveness goals, you should:

- Increase the quality of products.

- Reduce the number of defects.

- Reduce the cost of production.

- Increase customer service.

- Reduce delivery time to the customer.

2.14.9.4 System Resource Approach

The systems resource approach focuses on input and the extent to which an organization can acquire the resources it needs. It sees an organization as an open system. It emphasizes inputs over output. It focuses on the organization's ability to obtain necessary resources from the environments outside the organization. That is, how it exploits its environment in the acquisition of scarce and valued resources. Managers are to consider the organization not only as a whole but as a part of a larger group as well. The idea is that any part of an organization's activities affects all other parts.

The system resource approach has the following benefits:

- Enhance the bargaining position of your organization.

- Understand the relationship among each one of the separate processes of your system and how they interrelate to form a complete system.

- Organize the system in order to achieve the goal in the most efficient way possible, with a clear plan that can be implemented by relevant parties.

2.15 Measure Organizational Effectiveness

As you apply your effectiveness strategies, you'll need to re-evaluate and keep track of progress on how effective the organization has become and how to improve. To measure your organization's effectiveness, follow these steps.

Check Feeder Sources: This means key paths and roles that you determine to lead to your next stage of the plan. If you are successful at one stage, you proceed on to the next. Skipping an essential stage to get to your goal may not give a permanent result.

Calibrate With Metrics: What are your key performance indicators (KPIs)? Choosing the right KPIs relies upon a good understanding of what is important to the organization. It is the monitoring and reporting process. Set new performance expectations and metrics to promote collaboration and deliver the required changes.

Activity Domain: These are the activities you're basing effectiveness on, like goal realization, stakeholder satisfaction, financial return, and employee loyalty. It also includes how successfully an organization meets its targets, and the speed in attaining the goal, cost-efficiency and productivity.

Perspective: Determine from whose perspective your organization's effectiveness will be measured. Will it be from the employee's perspective? Customer perspective? Shareholders', societal, or employee perspective?

2.15.1 Level of Analysis

Measure the impact of your strategies on the individual, group, departmental, organization and industry level.

Time Frame: What is the time frame used for the analysis? Set a time frame for achieving your goals. For instance, measure the time spent on various stages of manufacturing before and after investing in the latest tech.

The Frame of Reference: How can you know you're succeeding at being effective? What can you compare your organization's present state with? Measure sales differentials before and after implementing an organization effectiveness strategy.

2.15.2 Strategies to Improve Organizational Effectiveness

Grant Autonomy at the Frontline: Employees need the freedom to carry out their work effectively. Empowering your team to make decisions without lengthy approval processes helps them develop and grow. Your employees need the right working environment to perform optimally. They should be able to act on their feet and deliver.

Recognition and Rewards: Reward people for jobs done well. Doing this encourages employees to continue behaving in the same way. It also enhances the sense of being a valued member of a group.

Clear and Defined Goals: Most organizations' goals are unclear. This makes their strategies and operating models to be misaligned, resulting in the delivery of substandard goals. Define where and how work gets done and get everyone on the same page.

Use Better Technology: Using advanced technology gives you a competitive edge. It makes things less complicated. Use suitable tools to keep teams updated. The tools and technology your organization uses will affect the organization. Select the right ones to execute tasks.

Improve the Employee Experience: How your employees act affects your company's productivity and output. If they have a good experience working for your organization, effectiveness will be improved. Fostering a healthy organization will make things flow smoothly for staff.

Increase Business Processes Efficiency: An improved business process will result in an improved organizational process. Seek business advice from professionals on how to improve your products and services. Discuss ways to reduce the time needed to hit your targets without reducing quality. Reduce waste by using better tools.

Focus on the Customer: Put your mind to serving your customers better. Request for them to fill in surveys. Encourage them to leave feedback on products and services provided. These steps will increase the quality of your products and services and help ensure that they meet your customers' expectations.

Exercise

1. What is innovation, and why is it considered a vital driver of entrepreneurial success and organizational growth?

2. Discuss the different types of innovation, including product innovation, process innovation, and business model innovation.

3. How does innovation contribute to competitive advantage and market differentiation for entrepreneurial ventures?

4. What are the key techniques and approaches for generating entrepreneurial ideas and identifying business opportunities?

5. How can entrepreneurs leverage market trends, consumer needs, and technological advancements to identify viable business opportunities?

6. Discuss the importance of creativity, problem-solving skills, and market research in entrepreneurial idea generation and opportunity recognition.

7. What are the essential management skills and competencies that entrepreneurs need to effectively lead and grow their ventures?

8. How do entrepreneurs manage resources, including human capital, financial resources, and strategic partnerships, to create value for their stakeholders?

9. Can you explain the concept of value creation and how entrepreneurs can measure and maximize value throughout the venture lifecycle?

10. What is an enterprising model, and how does it differ from traditional business models in terms of innovation, agility, and customer-centricity?

11. How do entrepreneurs create and sustain enterprising models that are adaptable to changing market conditions and customer preferences?

12. Discuss the importance of organizational effectiveness in driving entrepreneurial success, including factors such as leadership, culture, and operational efficiency.

Unit – 3

Project Management

Project Management: meaning, scope & importance, role of project manager; project life-cycle Project appraisal: Preparation of a real time project feasibility report containing Technical appraisal; Environmental appraisal, Market appraisal (including market survey for forecasting future demand and sales) and Managerial appraisal.

3.1 Meaning of Project Management

Project management is the discipline of planning, organizing, leading, and controlling resources to achieve specific goals and objectives within a defined timeframe and budget. It involves coordinating various tasks, activities, and stakeholders to ensure successful completion of a project. Project management encompasses a range of methodologies, tools, and techniques to effectively manage projects from initiation to closure.

- *Scope:* The scope of project management covers all aspects of a project's lifecycle.

- *Initiation:* Defining the project objectives, scope, stakeholders, and deliverables. This phase involves establishing the project's feasibility and obtaining approval to proceed.

- *Planning:* Developing a comprehensive project plan that outlines the project scope, schedule, budget, resources, quality requirements, risk management strategies, and communication protocols. Planning involves creating a roadmap to guide project execution and ensure alignment with organizational goals.

- *Execution:* Implementing the project plan by allocating resources, coordinating tasks, monitoring progress, and managing stakeholder expectations. Execution involves leading the project team, resolving issues, and adapting to changes to keep the project on track.

- *Monitoring and Controlling:* Tracking project performance against the planned objectives, schedule, and budget. Monitoring involves measuring progress, identifying variances, and implementing corrective actions to address deviations from the plan. Controlling ensures that the project stays within scope, schedule, and budget constraints while meeting quality standards.

- *Closure:* Formalizing project completion, delivering final deliverables to stakeholders, and conducting a post-project evaluation to assess lessons learned and identify areas for improvement. Closure involves documenting project outcomes, obtaining feedback from stakeholders, and transitioning any remaining responsibilities to the appropriate parties.

3.2 Importance of Project Management

Project management is essential for several reasons:

- *Achieving Goals:* Effective project management ensures that projects are completed on time, within budget, and to the required quality standards, enabling organizations to achieve their strategic objectives and deliver value to stakeholders.

- *Resource Optimization:* Project management helps optimize the use of resources, including human resources, financial resources, materials, and equipment, by allocating them efficiently and effectively to tasks and activities.

- ***Risk Management:*** Project management involves identifying, assessing, and mitigating risks that may impact project success. By proactively managing risks, project managers can minimize disruptions, avoid costly delays, and enhance project outcomes.

- ***Stakeholder Engagement:*** Project management facilitates communication and collaboration among project stakeholders, including team members, clients, sponsors, and other relevant parties. Effective stakeholder engagement ensures alignment of expectations, fosters trust, and promotes stakeholder satisfaction.

- ***Adaptability and Flexibility:*** Project management methodologies, such as Agile and Scrum, emphasize adaptability and flexibility, allowing teams to respond quickly to changes in requirements, priorities, and market conditions. This enables organizations to stay competitive and deliver value in dynamic environments.

- ***Continuous Improvement:*** Project management promotes a culture of continuous improvement by encouraging reflection, learning, and innovation. Lessons learned from past projects are documented and incorporated into future projects, leading to increased efficiency, productivity, and effectiveness over time.

3.3 User Roles of Project Manager

Project managers play various roles throughout the lifecycle of a project. These roles may vary depending on the size, complexity, and nature of the project, as well as the organizational context. Here are some of the key roles performed by project managers:

- ***Leader:*** Project managers serve as leaders who provide direction, guidance, and motivation to project team members. They inspire and empower team members to achieve project goals, foster collaboration, and maintain a positive working environment.

- ***Communicator:*** Effective communication is essential for project success, and project managers serve as primary communicators within the project team and with external stakeholders. They facilitate communication channels, ensure clarity of project objectives, disseminate information, and address concerns or issues in a timely manner.

- *Planner:* Project managers are responsible for developing comprehensive project plans that outline the project scope, objectives, deliverables, schedule, budget, resources, and risk management strategies. They create a roadmap to guide project execution and ensure alignment with organizational goals and stakeholder expectations.

- *Organizer:* Project managers organize and coordinate all aspects of the project, including tasks, activities, resources, and schedules. They allocate resources effectively, assign responsibilities to team members, and establish workflows and processes to streamline project execution.

- *Decision-maker:* Project managers make critical decisions throughout the project lifecycle, ranging from scope changes and resource allocation to risk mitigation strategies and issue resolution. They analyze data, assess options, and make informed decisions that align with project objectives and priorities.

- *Problem-solver:* Projects inevitably encounter challenges and obstacles, and project managers are tasked with identifying and resolving issues to keep the project on track. They anticipate potential problems, implement corrective actions, and collaborate with stakeholders to find practical solutions.

- *Risk Manager:* Project managers are responsible for identifying, assessing, and managing risks that may impact project success. They develop risk management plans, prioritize risks based on their likelihood and impact, and implement mitigation strategies to minimize threats and capitalize on opportunities.

- *Negotiator:* Project managers often engage in negotiations with stakeholders, team members, vendors, and other parties to resolve conflicts, reach consensus, and secure resources or support for the project. They use negotiation skills to achieve mutually beneficial outcomes and overcome obstacles.

- ***Quality Assurance:*** Project managers ensure that project deliverables meet the required quality standards and satisfy stakeholder expectations. They establish quality assurance processes, conduct regular inspections and reviews, and implement corrective actions to address deficiencies and improve quality.

- ***Change Agent:*** Projects often involve change within an organization, and project managers serve as change agents who facilitate the adoption of new processes, technologies, or practices. They communicate the rationale for change, address resistance, and support stakeholders in adapting to new ways of working.

- ***Client Liaison:*** Project managers act as the primary point of contact for clients or customers, representing their interests and ensuring that project deliverables meet their expectations. They manage client relationships, address concerns, and provide regular updates on project progress.

- ***Evaluator:*** After project completion, project managers conduct post-project evaluations to assess performance, identify lessons learned, and capture best practices. They document project outcomes, analyze project metrics, and compile reports for stakeholders, enabling continuous improvement and knowledge sharing.

3.4 Project Life Cycle

The Project Lifecycle consists of seven phases intake, initiation, planning, product selection, execution, monitoring & control, and closure. These phases make up the path that takes your project from start to finish.

- ***Intake Life Cycle:*** Project Intake is a process of reviewing and evaluating a proposed project during the initiation phase. The purpose is to confirm that the project is feasible and aims to address the stated problem. The process is also intended to review the organizational structure of the proposed project to define whether allocated human resources are sufficient and available for doing the project and producing desired deliverables.

- *Initiation:* This process helps in the visualization of what is to be accomplished. This is where the project is formally approved by the sponsor/client, initial scope defined, and stakeholders identified.

- *Planning:* The planning stage is where the project plans are documented, the project deliverables and requirements are defined, and the project schedule is created. It involves creating a set of plans to help guide your team through the implementation and closure phases of the project.

- *Product Selection:* This process refers to the selection, evaluation, and procurement of IT software that will be used and consumed in the project delivery.

- *Execution - Implementation:* This process is also known as the implementation phase, in which the plan designed in the previous phase of the project activity cycle is put into action. The intent of the execution phase of the project activity cycle is to bring about the project's expected results. Normally, this is the longest phase of the project management life cycle, where most resources are applied.

- *Monitoring and Control:* This process oversees all the tasks and metrics needed to guarantee that the agreed and approved project that is undertaken is within scope, on time and within budget so that the project proceeds with minimum risk.

- *Close:* This is considered to be the last process of the project activity cycle. In this stage, the project is formally closed and then a report is produced to the project sponsor/client on the overall level of success of the completed project.

3.5 Project Appraisal

Project appraisal is the process of evaluating the feasibility, viability, and potential outcomes of a proposed project before its initiation or implementation. It involves assessing various aspects of the project, including its objectives, scope, costs, benefits, risks, and overall impact. Project appraisal helps decision-makers make informed choices about whether to precede with a project, allocate resources, and determine the best course of action.

Key components of project appraisal typically include:

- ***Feasibility Analysis:*** This involves evaluating the technical, operational, and economic feasibility of the project. It assesses whether the project can be realistically implemented within the constraints of available resources, technology, and expertise.

- ***Cost-Benefit Analysis:*** Cost-benefit analysis compares the expected costs of the project with its anticipated benefits to determine whether the project is economically viable. It quantifies both the tangible and intangible costs and benefits associated with the project and calculates the net present value (NPV), return on investment (ROI), or other financial metrics to assess its economic viability.

- ***Risk Assessment:*** Project appraisal includes identifying and evaluating potential risks and uncertainties that may affect the project's success. This involves analyzing internal and external factors that could impact the project timeline, budget, quality, and outcomes, and developing risk management strategies to mitigate or manage these risks.

- ***Market Analysis:*** For projects with a commercial or market-oriented focus, project appraisal includes analyzing market dynamics, demand trends, competitive landscape, and customer preferences. This helps assess the market potential for the project's products or services and informs decisions about market positioning, pricing, and marketing strategies.

- ***Technical Evaluation:*** In projects involving technological innovation or complex technical requirements, technical evaluation assesses the technical feasibility and readiness of the proposed solution. It examines the technical specifications, capabilities, and limitations of the proposed technology or system and identifies any technical challenges or constraints that need to be addressed.

- ***Environmental and Social Impact Assessment:*** Project appraisal considers the potential environmental and social impacts of the project on the surrounding communities, ecosystems, and stakeholders. It evaluates the project's compliance with environmental regulations, social responsibility standards, and sustainability criteria, and identifies measures to minimize adverse impacts and enhance positive outcomes.

- ***Legal and Regulatory Compliance:*** Project appraisal examines the legal and regulatory requirements applicable to the project, including permits, licenses, zoning restrictions, and contractual obligations. It ensures that the project complies with all relevant laws, regulations, and industry standards and avoids potential legal liabilities or regulatory penalties.

- ***Stakeholder Analysis:*** Project appraisal identifies and analyzes the key stakeholders affected by or involved in the project, including internal and external stakeholders such as investors, customers, employees, suppliers, and government agencies. It assesses their interests, concerns, and influence on the project and develops strategies to engage and manage stakeholder relationships effectively.

3.6 Preparation of a Real Time Project Feasibility Report Containing Technical Appraisal

Preparing a feasibility report for a real-time project involves several steps, including technical appraisal. Here's a structured approach to creating such a report with a focus on technical appraisal:

1. Executive Summary

- Brief overview of the project.

- Summary of key findings from the feasibility study.

- Recommendation on whether to proceed with the project.

2. Introduction

- Background information on the project.

- Objectives and scope of the feasibility study.

- Overview of the project's technical aspects.

3. Project Description

- Detailed description of the project, including its purpose, goals, and deliverables.

- Description of the technical components involved in the project.

4. Technical Requirements

- Identification of the technical requirements needed to implement the project.

- Hardware, software, and other technical resources required.

- Technical specifications and standards to be followed.

5. Technical Feasibility

- Assessment of the technical feasibility of the project.

- Evaluation of whether the project can be implemented using available technology and resources.

- Analysis of any technical challenges or constraints that may impact project success.

6. Technical Approach

- Description of the proposed technical approach for implementing the project.

- Outline of the methodologies, technologies, and tools to be used.

- Overview of the project's architecture and design.

7. Risk Assessment

- Identification of technical risks and uncertainties associated with the project.

- Analysis of potential technical challenges, such as technological limitations, compatibility issues, or security concerns.

- Mitigation strategies for addressing technical risks and minimizing their impact on project outcomes.

8. Resource Requirements

- Assessment of the technical resources needed to execute the project.

- Evaluation of human resources, skills, and expertise required.

- Estimation of time, effort, and costs associated with technical activities.

9. Technical Evaluation Criteria

- Development of criteria for evaluating the technical aspects of the project.

- Criteria may include scalability, reliability, performance, security, and compliance with technical standards.

10. Conclusion and Recommendations

- Summary of the technical appraisal findings.

- Recommendation on the feasibility of the project from a technical perspective.

- Suggestions for next steps, such as further development, modifications, or alternative approaches.

11. Appendices

- Supporting documentation, technical specifications, diagrams, and other relevant materials.

12. References:

- Citations and references for sources used in the feasibility study.

13. Acknowledgments

- Recognition of individuals or organizations that contributed to the feasibility study.

By following this structured approach, you can create a comprehensive feasibility report that includes a thorough technical appraisal of the real-time project. This will help stakeholders make informed decisions about the project's viability and potential for success from a technical standpoint.

3.7 Technical Appraisal and Environmental Appraisal

Let's delve into the details of technical appraisal and environmental appraisal within the context of a feasibility report:

1. ***Technical Appraisal:*** Technical appraisal involves evaluating the technical feasibility and requirements of the proposed project. Here's how you can structure this section:

a. Technical Feasibility:

- Assess the feasibility of implementing the project from a technical perspective. Consider factors such as the availability of required technology, equipment, and expertise.

- Evaluate whether the project can be executed within the constraints of available resources and technology.

b. Technical Requirements:

- Specify the technical requirements needed for project implementation. This includes hardware, software, infrastructure, and other technical resources.

- Detail any specific technical standards, protocols, or regulations that must be adhered to.

c. Technology Assessment:

- Conduct an assessment of the proposed technology or methodologies to be used in the project.

- Evaluate the reliability, scalability, compatibility, and performance of the technology.

d. Risk Analysis:

- Identify potential technical risks and challenges that may arise during project execution.

- Assess the impact of technical risks on project objectives, schedule, and budget.

- Develop risk mitigation strategies to address identified technical risks and minimize their impact.

2. ***Environmental Appraisal:*** Environmental appraisal involves assessing the potential environmental impacts and considerations associated with the project. Here's how you can structure this section:

a. Environmental Impact Assessment (EIA):

- Conduct an environmental impact assessment to identify potential environmental risks and impacts associated with the project.

- Evaluate the project's potential effects on air quality, water resources, land use, biodiversity, and ecosystems.

b. Regulatory Compliance:

- Assess the project's compliance with environmental regulations, laws, and standards at the local, regional, and national levels.

- Identify any permits, licenses, or approvals required for the project and ensure compliance with relevant environmental legislation.

c. Mitigation Measures:

- Develop mitigation measures and environmental management strategies to minimize adverse environmental impacts.

- Identify measures to prevent pollution, conserve natural resources, and promote environmental sustainability.

d. Stakeholder Engagement:

- Engage with stakeholders, including local communities, environmental agencies, and non-governmental organizations (NGOs), to address their concerns and obtain input on environmental issues.

- Foster transparency and communication regarding the project's environmental aspects and potential impacts.

e. Monitoring and Reporting:

- Establish monitoring and reporting mechanisms to track environmental performance throughout the project lifecycle.

- Implement regular environmental monitoring and reporting to assess compliance with environmental requirements and identify opportunities for improvement.

3.8 Market Appraisal (Including Market Survey for Forecasting Future Demand and Sales)

Market appraisal, including conducting a market survey for forecasting future demand and sales, is a crucial aspect of the feasibility report. Here's how you can structure this section:

1. ***Market Overview:*** Provide an overview of the market in which the proposed project will operate. This includes:

   - Description of the target market segments.

   - Analysis of market trends, growth drivers, and challenges.

   - Identification of key competitors and their market positions.

2. ***Market Research Methodology:***

   - Describe the methodology used to conduct the market survey. This may include:

   - ***Sampling approach:*** Explain how the sample population was selected for the survey.

   - ***Data collection methods:*** Specify the techniques used to gather data, such as surveys, interviews, or secondary research.

   - ***Survey instruments:*** Detail the survey questions, formats, and instruments used to collect market data.

3. ***Market Survey Findings:***

   - Present the findings of the market survey, focusing on key metrics and insights. This may include:

- ***Demand analysis:*** Assess current market demand for products or services similar to those offered by the proposed project.

- ***Customer preferences:*** Identify customer preferences, needs, and buying behaviors relevant to the project.

- ***Competitive analysis:*** Evaluate the competitive landscape, including market share, pricing strategies, and strengths/weaknesses of competitors.

- ***Market segmentation:*** Segment the market based on demographic, geographic, psychographic, or behavioral factors.

- ***Sales forecasting:*** Use survey data and market trends to forecast future demand and sales for the proposed project.

4. ***Demand Forecasting:***

- Use the survey findings and market analysis to forecast future demand for the project's products or services. This involves:

- ***Quantitative analysis:*** Use statistical techniques to extrapolate current demand trends and predict future market demand.

- ***Scenario analysis:*** Consider different scenarios and assumptions to assess the range of possible outcomes for demand forecasting.

- ***Sensitivity analysis:*** Identify key variables and factors that may influence demand forecasts and analyze their impact on projections.

5. ***Sales Forecasting:*** Based on the forecasted demand, estimate future sales for the project. This includes:

- ***Sales projections:*** Estimate sales volumes and revenues over a specified time period (e.g., monthly, quarterly, annually).

- ***Pricing strategy:*** Determine pricing strategies based on market demand, competitor pricing, and cost considerations.

- ***Sales channels:*** Identify distribution channels and sales channels through which the project's products or services will be marketed and sold.

6. ***Market Strategy:*** Develop a market strategy based on the market appraisal findings. This may include:

   - ***Positioning strategy:*** Define the project's unique value proposition and positioning within the market.

   - ***Marketing tactics:*** Outline marketing tactics and activities to reach target customers and promote the project's offerings.

   - ***Market penetration:*** Identify strategies to penetrate the market and gain market share, such as pricing promotions, advertising campaigns, or partnerships.

7. ***Conclusion and Recommendations:*** Summarize the findings of the market appraisal and provide recommendations based on the market analysis. This includes:

   - Assessment of market feasibility and attractiveness.

   - Recommendations on market entry strategies and opportunities.

   - Suggestions for adapting the project's offerings or marketing approach based on market insights.

3.9 Demand Forecasting

An important aspect of demand analysis from the management point of view is concerned with forecasting demand for products, either existing or new. Demand forecasting refers to an estimate of most likely future demand for product under given conditions. Such forecasts are of immense use in making decisions with regard to production, sales, investment, expansion, employment of manpower etc., both in the short run as well as in the long run.

3.9.1 Meaning and Features of Demand Forecasting

Demand forecasting seeks to investigate and measure the forces that determine sales for existing and new products. Generally companies plan their business – production or sales in anticipation of future demand. Hence forecasting future demand becomes important. In fact it is the very soul of good business because every business decision is based on some assumptions about the future whether right or wrong, implicit or explicit. The art of successful business lies in avoiding or minimizing the risks involved as far as possible and face the uncertainties in a most befitting manner .Thus Demand Forecasting refers to an estimation of most likely future demand for a product under given conditions.

Important features of demand forecasting

- It is basically a guess work – but it is an educated and well thought out guesswork.

- It is in terms of specific quantities

- It is undertaken in an uncertain atmosphere.

- A forecast is made for a specific period of time which would be sufficient to take a decision and put it into action.

- It is based on historical information and the past data.

- It tells us only the approximate demand for a product in the future.

- It is based on certain assumptions.

- It cannot be 100% precise as it deals with future expected demand

Demand forecasting is needed to know whether the demand is subject to cyclical fluctuations or not, so that the production and inventory policies, etc, can be suitably formulated

Demand forecasting is generally associated with forecasting sales and manipulating demand. A firm can make use of the sales forecasts made by the industry as a powerful tool for formulating sales policy and sales strategy. They can become action guides to select the course of action which will maximize the firm's earnings. When external economic factors like the size of market, competitors attitudes, movement in prices, consumer tastes, possibilities of new threats from substitute products etc., influence sales forecasting, internal factors like money spent on advertising, pricing policy, product improvements, sales efforts etc., help in manipulating demand. To use demand forecasting in an active rather than a passive way, management must recognize the degree to which sales are a result not only of external economic environment but also of the action of the company itself.

3.9.2 Managerial Uses of Demand Forecasting:

In the short run: Demand forecasts for short periods are made on the assumption that the company has a given production capacity and the period is too short to change the existing production capacity. Generally it would be one year period.

- *Production planning:* It helps in determining the level of output at various periods and avoiding under or over production.

- *Helps to formulate right purchase policy:* It helps in better material management, of buying inputs and control its inventory level which cuts down cost of operation.

- *Helps to frame realistic pricing policy:* A rational pricing policy can be formulated to suit short run and seasonal variations in demand.

- ***Sales forecasting:*** It helps the company to set realistic sales targets for each individual salesman and for the company as a whole.

- ***Helps in estimating short run financial requirements:*** It helps the company to plan the finances required for achieving the production and sales targets. The company will be able to raise the required finance well in advance at reasonable rates of interest.

- ***Reduce the dependence on chances:*** The firm would be able to plan its production properly and face the challenges of competition efficiently.

- Helps to evolve a suitable Labor policy: A proper sales and production policies help to determine the exact number of Laborers to be employed in the short run.

In the long run: Long run forecasting of probable demand for a product of a company is generally for a period of 3 to 5 or 10 years.

- ***Business planning:*** It helps to plan expansion of the existing unit or a new production unit. Capital budgeting of a firm is based on long run demand forecasting.

- ***Financial planning:*** It helps to plan long run financial requirements and investment programs by floating shares and debentures in the open market.

- ***Manpower planning:*** It helps in preparing long term planning for imparting training to the existing staff and recruit skilled and efficient Labor force for its long run growth.

- ***Business control:*** Effective control over total costs and revenues of a company helps to determine the value and volume of business. This in its turn helps to estimate the total profits of the firm. Thus it is possible to regulate business effectively to meet the challenges of the market.

- ***Determination of the growth rate of the firm:*** A steady and well-conceived demand forecasting determine the speed at which the company can grow.

- ***Establishment of stability in the working of the firm :*** Fluctuations in production cause ups and downs in business which retards smooth functioning of the firm. Demand forecasting reduces production uncertainties and help in stabilizing the activities of the firm.

- ***Indicates interdependence of different industries:*** Demand forecasts of particular products become the basis for demand forecasts of other related industries, e.g., demand forecast for cotton textile industry supply information to the most likely demand for textile machinery, colour, dye-stuff industry etc.

3.9.3 Levels of Demand Forecasting

Demand forecasting may be undertaken at three different levels, viz., micro level or firm level,industry level and macro level.

- ***Micro level or firm level:*** This refers to the demand forecasting by the firm for its product. The management of a firm is really interested in such forecasting. Generally speaking, demand forecasting refers to the forecasting of demand of a firm.

- ***Industry level:*** Demand forecasting for the product of an industry as a whole is generally undertaken by the trade associations and the results are made available to the members. A member firm by using such data and information may determine its market share.

- ***Macro-level:*** Estimating industry demand for the economy as a whole will be based on macro-economic variables like national income, national expenditure, consumption function, index of industrial production, aggregate demand, aggregate supply etc, Generally, it is undertaken by national institutes, govt. agencies etc. Such forecasts are helpful to the Government in determining the volume of exports and imports, control of prices etc. The managerial economist has to take into consideration the estimates of aggregate demand and also industry demand while making the demand forecast for the product of a particular firm.

3.9.4 Criteria for Good Demand Forecasting

Apart from being technically efficient and economically ideal a good method of demand forecasting should satisfy a few broad economic criteria. They are as follows:

- *Accuracy:* Accuracy is the most important criterion of a demand forecast, even though cent percent accuracy about the future demand cannot be assured. It is generally measured in terms of the past forecasts on the present sales and by the number of times it is correct.

- *Plausibility:* The techniques used and the assumptions made should be intelligible to the management. It is essential for a correct interpretation of the results.

- *Simplicity:* It should be simple, reasonable and consistent with the existing knowledge. A simple method is always more comprehensive than the complicated one

- *Durability:* Durability of demand forecast depends on the relationships of the variables considered and the stability underlying such relationships, as for instance, the relation between price and demand, between advertisement and sales, between the level of income and the volume of sales, and so on.

- *Flexibility:* There should be scope for adjustments to meet the changing conditions. This imparts durability to the technique.

- *Availability of data:* Immediate availability of required data is of vital importance to business. It should be made available on an up-to-date basis. There should be scope for making changes in the demand relationships as they occur.

- ***Economy:*** It should involve lesser costs as far as possible. Its costs must be compared against the benefits of forecasts

- ***Quickness:*** It should be capable of yielding quick and useful results. This helps the management to take quick and effective decisions.

3.10 Analyze Different Methods Demand Forecasting for both Old and New Products

Demand forecasting is a highly complicated process as it deals with the estimation of future demand. It requires the assistance and opinion of experts in the field of sales management. While estimating future demand, one should not give too much of importance to either statistical information, past data or experience, intelligence and judgment of the experts. Demand forecasting, to become more realistic should consider the two aspects in a balanced manner. Application of common sense is needed to follow a pragmatic approach in demand forecasting.

Broadly speaking, there are two methods of demand forecasting. They are: 1.Survey methods and 2 Statistical methods.

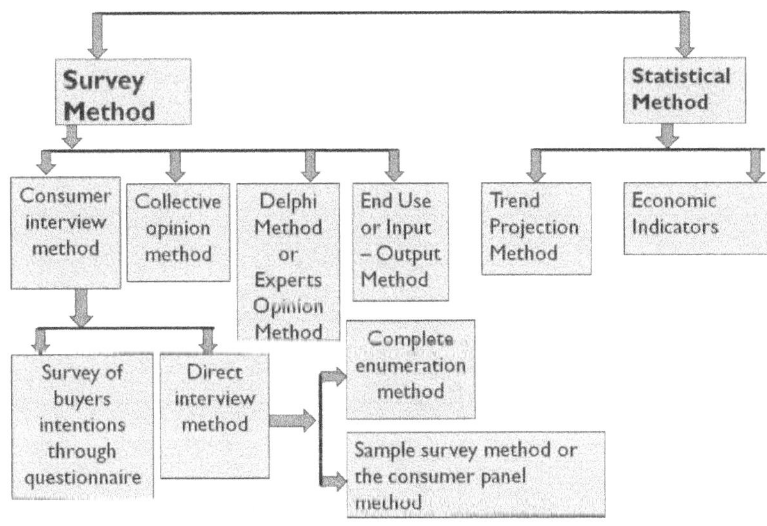

3.10.1 Survey Methods

Survey methods help us in obtaining information about the future purchase plans of potential buyers through collecting the opinions of experts or by interviewing the consumers. These methods are extensively used in short run and estimating the demand for new products. There are different approaches under survey methods. They are:

3.10.1.1 Consumers interview Method:

Under this method, efforts are made to collect the relevant information directly from the consumers with regard to their future purchase plans. In order to gather information from consumers, a number of alternative techniques are developed from time to time. Among them, the following are some of the important ones.

3.10.1.1.1 Survey of buyer's intentions or preferences:

It is one of the oldest methods of demand forecasting. It is also called as "Opinion surveys".

Under this method, consumer-buyers are requested to indicate their preferences and willingness about particular products. They are asked to reveal their 'future purchase plans with respect to specific items. They are expected to give answers to questions like what items they intend to buy, in what quantity, why, where, when, what quality they expect, how much money they are planning to spend etc. Generally, the field survey is conducted by the marketing research department of the company or hiring the services of outside research organizations consisting of learned and highly qualified professionals.

The heart of the survey is questionnaire. It is a comprehensive one covering almost all questions either directly or indirectly in a most intelligent manner. It is prepared by an expert body who are specialists in the field or marketing.

The questionnaire is distributed among the consumer buyers either through mail or in person by the company. Consumers are requested to furnish all relevant and correct information.

The next step is to collect the questionnaire from the consumers for the purpose of evaluation. The materials collected will be classified, edited analyzed. If any bias prejudices, exaggerations, artificial or excess demand creation etc., are found at the time of answering they would be eliminated.

The information so collected will now be consolidated and reviewed by the top executives with lot of experience. It will be examined thoroughly. Inferences are drawn and conclusions are arrived at. Finally a report is prepared and submitted to management for taking final decisions.

The success of the survey method depends on many factors.

1. The nature of the questions asked,

2. The ability of the surveyed

3. The representative of the samples

4. Nature of the product

5. Characteristics of the market

6. Consumer buyer's behavior, their intentions, attitudes, thoughts, motives, honesty etc.

7. Techniques of analysis conclusions drawn etc.

The management should not entirely depend on the results of survey reports to project future demand. Consumer buyers may not express their honest and real views and as such they may give only the broad trends in the market. In order to arrive at right conclusions, field surveys should be regularly checked and supervised.

This method is simple and useful to the producers who produce goods in bulk. Here the burden of forecasting is put on customers.

However this method is not much useful in estimating the future demand of the households as they run in large numbers and also do not freely express their future demand requirements. It is expensive and also difficult. Preparation of a questionnaire is not an easy task. At best it can be used for short term forecasting.

3.10.1.1.2 Direct Interview Method

Experience has shown that many customers do not respond to questionnaire addressed to them even if it is simple due to varied reasons. Hence, an alternative method is developed. Under this method, customers are directly contacted and interviewed. Direct and simple questions are asked to them. They are requested to answer specifically about their budget, expenditure plans, particular items to be selected, the quality and quantity of products, relative price preferences etc. for a particular period of time. There are two different methods of direct personal interviews. They are as follows:

3.10.1.1.2.1 Complete enumeration method

Under this method, all potential customers are interviewed in a particular city or a region. The answers elicited are consolidated and carefully studied to obtain the most probable demand for a product. The management can safely project the future demand for its products. This method is free from all types of prejudices. The result mainly depends on the nature of questions asked and answers received from the customers.

However, this method cannot be used successfully by all sellers in all cases. This method can be employed to only those products whose customers are concentrated in a small region or locality. In case consumers are widely dispersed, this method may not be physically adopted or prove costly both in terms of time and money. Hence, this method is highly cumbersome in nature.

3.10.1.1.2.2 Sample survey method or the consumer panel method

Experience of the experts" show that it is impossible to approach all customers; as such careful sampling of representative customers is essential. Hence, another variant of complete enumeration method has been developed, which is popularly known as sample survey method. Under this method, different cross sections of customers that make up the bulk of the market are carefully chosen. Only such consumers selected from the relevant market through some sampling method are interviewed or surveyed. In other words, a group of consumers are chosen and queried about their preferences in concrete situations. The selection of a few customers is known as sampling. The selected consumers form a panel. This method uses either random sampling or the stratified sampling technique. The method of survey may be direct interview or mailed questionnaire to the selected consumers. On the basis of the views expressed by these selected consumers, most likely demand may be estimated. The advantage of a panel lies in the fact that the same panel is continued and new expensive panel does not have to be formulated every time a new product is investigated.

As compared to the complete enumeration method, the sample survey method is less tedious, less expensive, much simpler and less time consuming. This method is generally used to estimate short run demand by government departments and business firms.

Success of this method depends upon the sincere co-operation of the selected customers. Hence, selection of suitable consumers for the specific purpose is of great importance.

Even with careful selection of customers and the truthful information about their buying intention, the results of the survey can only be of limited use. A sudden change in price, inconsistency in buying intentions of consumers, number of sensible questions asked and dropouts from the panel for various reasons put a serious limitation on the practical usefulness of the panel method.

3.10.1.2 Collective opinion Method or Opinion Survey Method

This is a variant of the survey method. This method is also known as "Sales – force polling" or "Opinion poll method". Under this method, sales representatives, professional experts and the market consultants and others are asked to express their considered opinions about the volume of sales expected in the future. The logic and reasoning behind the method is that these salesmen and other people connected with the sales department are directly involved in the marketing and selling of the products in different regions. Salesmen, being very close to the customers, will be in a position to know and feel the customer"s reactions towards the product. They can study the pulse of the people and identify the specific views of the customers. These people are quite capable of estimating the likely demand for the products with the help of their intimate and friendly contact with the customers and their personal judgments based on the past experience. Thus, they provide approximate, if not accurate estimates. Then, the views of all salesmen are aggregated to get the overall probable demand for a product.

Further, these opinions or estimates collected from the various experts are considered, consolidated and reviewed by the top executives to eliminate the bias or optimism and pessimism of different salesmen. These revised estimates are further examined in the light of factors like proposed change in selling prices, product designs and advertisement programs, expected changes in the degree of competition, income distribution, population etc. The final sales forecast would emerge after these factors have been taken into account. This method heavily depends on the collective wisdom of salesmen, departmental heads and the top executives.

The main drawback is that it is subjective and depends on the intelligence and awareness of the salesmen. It cannot be relied upon for long term business planning.

3.10.1.3 Delphi Method or Experts Opinion Method

This method was originally developed at Rand Corporation in the late 1940"s by Olaf Helmer, Dalkey and Gordon. This method was used to predict future technological changes. It has proved more useful and popular in forecasting non– economic rather than economic variables.

It is a variant of opinion poll and survey method of demand forecasting. Under this method, outside experts are appointed. They are supplied with all kinds of information and statistical data. The management requests the experts to express their considered opinions and views about the expected future sales of the company. Their views are generally regarded as most objective ones. Their views generally avoid or reduce the "Halo – Effects" and "Ego – Involvement" of the views of the others. Since experts" opinions are more valuable, a firm will give lot of importance to them and prepare their future plan on the basis of the forecasts made by the experts.

3.10.1.4 End Use or Input – Output Method

Under this method, the sale of the product under consideration is projected on the basis of demand surveys of the industries using the given product as an intermediate product. The demand for the final product is the end – use demand of the intermediate product used in the production of the final product. An intermediate product may have many end users, For e.g., steel can be used for making various types of agricultural and industrial machinery, for construction, for transportation etc. It may have the demand both in the domestic market as well as international market. Thus, end – use demand estimation of an intermediate product may involve many final goods industries using this product, at home and abroad. Once we know the demand for final consumption goods including their exports we can estimate the demand for the product which is used as intermediate good in the production of these final goods with the help of input – output coefficients. The input – output table containing input – output coefficients for particular periods are made available in every country either by the Government or by research organizations.

This method is used to forecast the demand for intermediate products only. It is quite useful for industries which are largely producers" goods, like aluminium, steel etc. The main limitation of the method is that as the number of end – users of a product increase, it becomes more inconvenient to use this method.

3.10.2 Statistical Method

It is the second most popular method of demand forecasting. It is the best available technique and most commonly used method in recent years. Under this method, statistical, mathematical models, equations etc are extensively used in order to estimate future demand of a particular product. They are used for estimating long term demand. They are highly complex and complicated in nature. Some of them require considerable mathematical back – ground and competence.

They use historical data in estimating future demand. The analysis of the past demand serves as the basis for present trends and both of them become the basis for calculating the future demand of a commodity in question after taking into account of likely changes in the future.

There are several statistical methods and their application should be done by someone who is reasonably well versed in the methods of statistical analysis and in the interpretation of the results of such analysis.

3.10.2.1 Trend Projection Method

An old firm operating in the market for a long period will have the accumulated previous data on either production or sales pertaining to different years. If we arrange them in chronological order, we get what is called as „time series" . It is an ordered sequence of events over a period of time pertaining to certain variables. It shows a series of values of a dependent variable say, sales as it changes from one point of time to another. In short, a time series is a set of observations taken at specified time, generally at equal intervals. It depicts the historical pattern under normal conditions. This method is not based on any particular theory as to what causes the variables to change but merely assumes that whatever forces contributed to change in the recent past will continue to have the same effect. On the basis of time series, it is possible to project the future sales of a company.

Further, the statistics and information with regard to the sales call for further analysis. When we represent the time series in the form of a graph, we get a curve, the sales curve. It shows the trend in sales at different periods of time. Also, it indicates fluctuations and turning points in demand. If the turning points are few and their intervals are also widely spread, they yield acceptable results. Here the time series show a persistent tendency to move in the same direction. Frequency in turning points indicates uncertain demand conditions and in this case, the trend projection breaks down.

The major task of a firm while estimating the future demand lies in the prediction of turning points in the business rather than in the projection of trends. When turning points occur more frequently, the firm has to make radical changes in its basic policy with respect to future demand. It is for this reason that the experts give importance to identification of turning points while projecting the future demand for a product.

The heart of this method lies in the use of time series. Changes in time series arise on account of the following reasons:

- ***Secular or long run movements:*** Secular movements indicate the general conditions and direction in which graph of a time series move in relatively a long period of time.

- ***Seasonal movements:*** Time series also undergo changes during seasonal sales of a company. During festival season, sales clearance season etc., we come across mostunexpected changes.

- ***Cyclical Movements:*** It implies change in time series or fluctuations in the demand for aproduct during different phases of a business cycle like depression, revival, boom etc.

- ***Random movement:*** When changes take place at random, we call them irregular or random movements. These movements imply sporadic changes in time series occurring due to unforeseen events such as floods, strikes, elections, earth quakes, droughts and other such natural calamities. Such changes take place only in the short run. Still they have their own impact on the sales of a company.

An important question in this connection is how to ascertain the trend in time series? A statistician, in order to find out the pattern of change in time series may make use of the following methods.

- The Least Squares method

- The Free hand method

- The moving average method

- The method of semi – averages

The method of Least Squares is more scientific, popular and thus more commonly used when compared to the other methods. It uses the straight line equation $Y = a + bx$ to fit the trend to the data.

3.10.2.2 Economic Indicators

- Economic indicators as a method of demand forecasting are developed recently. Under this method, a few economic indicators become the basis for forecasting the sales of a company. An economic indicator indicates change in the magnitude of an economic variable. It gives the signal about the direction of change in an economic variable. This helps in decision making process of a company. We can mention a few economic indicators in this context.

- Construction contracts sanctioned for demand towards building materials like cement.

- Personal income towards demand for consumer goods.

- Agriculture income towards the demand for agricultural in puts, instruments, fertilizers, manure, etc,

- Automobile registration towards demand for car spare parts, petrol etc.,

- Personal Income, Consumer Price Index, Money supply etc., towards demand for consumption goods.

3.11 Demand Forecasting For A New Product

Demand forecasting for new products is quite different from that for established products. Here the firms will not have any past experience or past data for this purpose. An intensive study of the economic and competitive characteristics of the product should be made to make efficient forecasts.

Professor Joel Dean, however, has suggested a few guidelines to make forecasting of demand for new products.

- ***Evolutionary approach:*** The demand for the new product may be considered as an outgrowth of an existing product. For e.g., Demand for new Tata Indica, which is a modified version of Old Indica can most effectively be projected based on the sales of the old Indica, the demand for new Pulsor can be forecasted based on the sales of the old Pulsor. Thus when a new product is evolved from the old product, the demand conditions of the old product can be taken as a basis for forecasting the demand for the new product.

- ***Substitute approach:*** If the new product developed serves as substitute for the existing product, the demand for the new product may be worked out on the basis of a „market share". The growths of demand for all the products have to be worked out on the basis of intelligent forecasts for independent variables that influence the demand for the substitutes. After that, a portion of the market can be sliced out for the new product. For e.g., A moped as a substitute for a scooter, a cell phone as a substitute for a land line. In some cases price plays an important role in shaping future demand for the product.

- ***Opinion Poll approach:*** Under this approach the potential buyers are directly contacted, or through the use of samples of the new product and their responses are found out. These are finally blown up to forecast the demand for the new product.

- ***Sales experience approach:*** Offer the new product for sale in a sample market; say supermarkets or big bazaars in big cities, which are also big marketing centers. The product may be offered for sale through one super market and the estimate of sales obtained may be „blown up" to arrive at estimated demand for the product.

- ***Growth Curve approach:*** According to this, the rate of growth and the ultimate level of demand for the new product are estimated on the basis of the pattern of growth of established products. For e.g., An Automobile Co., while introducing a new version of a car will study the level of demand for the existing car.

- ***Vicarious approach:*** A firm will survey consumers" reactions to a new product indirectly through getting in touch with some specialized and informed dealers who have good knowledge about the market, about the different varieties of the product already available in the market, the consumers" preferences etc. This helps in making a more efficient estimation of future demand.

3.12 Managerial Appraisal

Harold Koontz has developed a concept of managerial appraisal i.e., appraising managers. According to this concept the managers attain the organizational objectives by performing the basic managerial functions, viz., planning, organizing, leading, motivating, staffing and controlling.

Each of these functions can be performed by performing a number of or series of activities.

For example, performing staffing function requires performing a series of activities like analyzing jobs of his department, planning for human resources, deciding upon internal and external recruitment, developing sources and recruitment techniques. Thus, each function and sub-function of manager is elaborated into a series of activities. These activities, in this model are taken as behavior and standards of performance. The checklist containing the questions in these areas is prepared with a five degree rating scale, i.e., extremely poor performance, neither poor nor fair performance and extremely fair performance.

The appraisers rate performance of managers by assessing weights to the scale and appraise only those areas which are clear and are supported by adequate knowledge. Thus, this technique measures the performance of managers in managing organizational environment.

3.12.1 Criteria for Managerial Appraisal

There are multiple perspectives for manager's appraisal, the most fundamental requirements for any appraiser is that appraiser has also adequate time and chances to observe the job performance of their subordinates. This requirement suggests several possible appraisers. (These are above, below, coequals and customers).

The Immediate Supervisor: Supervisor is the person who is taking care of the own job and actually knowing who all are performing and how they are performing because the person who is directly observing the performance of his subordinates, so he must carry out the appraisal of his own subordinates.

Peers: In some jobs such as outside sales in some environment such as self-manage work teams, the immediate supervisor may observe a subordinates actual job performance only rarely (indirectly through written reports).Peers can provide a perspective on performance that is different from that of immediate supervisor. So the peer assessment is the best approach through which performance of an individual is being judged by incorporating input from all resources.

Subordinates: Appraisal by subordinates can be a use full input to the immediate supervisors' developments, subordinates know first hand the extent to which the supervisor actually delegates and how well he or she communicate the type of leadership style, plan and organize the work. The progress of an establishment is directly related to all this. So, upper manger get the reports about the supervisors through various means.

Self-Appraisal: Self-appraisal is opportunity to participate in the performance appraisal process particularly if the appraisal is combined with the goal setting improves the rate's motivation and reduces his or her defensiveness during the appraisal interview. The different procedure is being adopted by the various organizations but actual it's difficult for a person to assess his own performance. This techniques may be used by some of senior executive may not be adopted commonly for all employees.

Customers Served: In some situations "consumers" of an individual or organization s services can provide a unique perspective of on job performance. Although the consumers objective can be different from the organizations, yet the information provided help the management to observe and develop the overall performance of the organization and it employees.

Computers: As noted earlier, employee spends a lot of time unsupervised by their bosses. Now technology has made continuous supervision possible to look after this very aspect comprehensively.

Exercise

1. What is the meaning of project management, and why is it considered crucial in achieving organizational objectives?

2. Discuss the scope of project management and how it encompasses planning, execution, monitoring, and control of projects.

3. Why is project management important in ensuring the successful delivery of projects within constraints such as time, cost, and quality?

4. What are the key responsibilities and roles of a project manager in overseeing and coordinating project activities?

5. Can you explain the concept of the project life cycle, including its phases and typical activities involved in each phase?

6. What is project appraisal, and why is it essential in evaluating the feasibility and viability of proposed projects?

7. Describe the components of a real-time project feasibility report, including technical, environmental, market, and managerial appraisals.

8. How is technical appraisal conducted in project appraisal, and what factors are considered in assessing the technical feasibility of a project?

9. Discuss the importance of environmental appraisal in project appraisal and how environmental impact assessments are conducted.

10. Explain the process of conducting market appraisal as part of project feasibility analysis, including methods for forecasting future demand and sales in the target market.

Unit – 4

Project Financing

Project Financing: Project cost estimation & working capital requirements, sources of funds, capital budgeting, Risk & uncertainty in project evaluation, preparation of projected financial statements viz. Projected balance sheet, projected income statement, projected funds & cash flow statements, Preparation of detailed project report, Project finance.

4.1 Project Financing

Project Finance can be characterised in a variety of ways and there is no universally adopted definition but as a financing technique, the author's definition is:

"the raising of finance on a Limited Recourse basis, for the purposes of developing a large capital- intensive infrastructure project, where the borrower is a special purpose vehicle and repayment of the financing by the borrower will be dependent on the internally generated cashflows of the project"

This definition in itself raises a number of interesting questions, including:

- What do we mean by 'Limited Recourse' financing – recourse to whom or what?

- Why Project Finance is typically used to finance large capital intensive infrastructure projects?

- Why is the borrower a special purpose vehicle (SPV) under a project financing?

- What happens if the internally generated cashflows of the project are not sufficient to repay the financiers of the project?

The terms 'Project Finance' and 'Limited Recourse Finance' are typically used interchangeably and should be viewed as one in the same. Indeed, it is debatable the extent to which a financing where the Lenders have significant collateral with (or other form of contractual remedy against) the project shareholders of the borrower can be truly regarded as a project financing. The 'limited' recourse that financiers have to a project's shareholders in a true project financing is a major motivation for corporates adopting this approach to infrastructure investment.

Project financing is largely an exercise in the equitable allocation of a project's risks between the various stakeholders of the project. Indeed, the genesis of the financing technique can be traced back to this principle. Roman and Greek merchants used project financing techniques in order to share the risks inherent to maritime trading. A loan would be advanced to a shipping merchant on the agreement that such loan would be repaid only through the sale of cargo brought back by the voyage (i.e. the financing would be repaid by the 'internally generated cashflows of the project', to use modern project financing terminology).

4.1.1 Advantages and Disadvantages of Project Financing

Here are the advantages and disadvantages of project financing:

Advantages:

- ***Limited Recourse:*** One of the primary advantages of project financing is that it typically involves limited recourse to the project sponsors or investors. If the project fails or encounters financial difficulties, the lenders' claims are usually limited to the project's assets and cash flows, protecting the sponsors' other assets.

- **Risk Allocation:** Project financing allows for the allocation of risks to parties best equipped to manage them. Lenders, equity investors, and other stakeholders assume specific risks based on their roles and expertise, reducing the overall risk exposure for individual parties.

- **Leverage:** Project financing enables projects to be undertaken with a higher degree of leverage, as lenders are primarily interested in the project's cash flow and assets rather than the sponsors' balance sheets. This allows projects to access larger amounts of capital than may be available through traditional financing methods.

- **Off-Balance Sheet Financing:** Project financing may allow sponsors to keep the project's debt off their balance sheets, improving their financial ratios and creditworthiness. This can be advantageous for sponsors seeking to maintain flexibility and access to additional financing for other projects or investments.

- **Customized Financing Structures:** Project financing offers flexibility in structuring financing arrangements to meet the specific needs of the project. Financing structures can be tailored to accommodate project risks, cash flow characteristics, and investor preferences, maximizing financial efficiency.

Disadvantages:

- **Complexity:** Project financing involves complex legal, financial, and contractual arrangements among multiple parties, including lenders, investors, sponsors, and contractors. Managing these complexities requires specialized expertise and may result in higher transaction costs and administrative burdens.

- **High Transaction Costs:** The structuring and negotiation of project financing arrangements can incur significant transaction costs, including legal fees, due diligence expenses, and financing fees. These costs may be prohibitive for smaller-scale projects or projects with uncertain financial viability.

- ***Higher Financing Costs:*** Project financing typically involves higher financing costs compared to traditional corporate financing. Lenders and investors may charge higher interest rates, fees, and equity returns to compensate for the project's perceived risks, complexity, and lack of recourse.

- ***Cash Flow Dependency:*** Project financing relies heavily on the project's cash flows to service debt and generate returns for investors. Any disruptions to the project's cash flow, such as delays, cost overruns, or revenue shortfalls, can increase the risk of default and financial distress.

- ***Limited Flexibility:*** Once project financing arrangements are in place, they may offer limited flexibility for sponsors to adapt to changing circumstances or market conditions. Restrictive covenants, financial ratios, and project milestones imposed by lenders and investors may constrain the sponsors' ability to modify project plans or seek alternative financing options.

4.1.2 Requirements for Project Financing

In case of project finance, no project history or past operating data is available. The creditworthiness of the project depends on projected profitability and indirect credit support provided by the sponsors, lenders, EPC and O&M contractors, raw material suppliers, off-take parties and the government. The lenders get comfort by having completion guarantees from the sponsors. The sponsors assure the lenders that project will be completed within stipulated time and cost framework. If it does not happen, the lenders will have recourse to sponsors' balance sheets for their claims. If project is completed within stipulated time and cost framework, thereafter lenders have no claim to the sponsors' balance sheets. Their claim will be met out of project cash flows and project assets. Thus, the lenders provide limited recourse finance during the construction period of the project and no-recourse finance to the project after its successful implementation

1. Technical Feasibility

The lenders want to satisfy themselves that the technology used for the project is proven technology, environmental friendly and is capable of operating at desired level of production. For this purpose, they need an opinion of independent consultants, and engineering firms.

2. Economic Viability

The lenders want to be assured that project will be put to operation successfully on stipulated date and will generate free cash flows to service the debt and provide the required rate of return to the sponsors after keeping reserves for operation and maintenance. Further, there should be long-term demand for the project output and there must be an off-take agreement with the customers.

3. Availability of Raw Materials

The raw materials and other inputs required to manufacture desired level of output over the life cycle of the project should be available. The project SPV may enter into an agreement with the raw material suppliers to share the input risk. If the project uses natural resources such as oil reserves in case of oil & gas project, bauxite reserves in case of aluminium project, the project SPV may enter into an agreement with the Government for use of natural resources over the life of the project.

4. Competent Management

The project entity must have competent management in place in order to ensure successful execution of the project. If it is not there, then Project SPV must enter into an agreement with the engineering firms. For example, in case of Hong Kong Disneyland Project, the project has to be operated by Disney against a management fee.

4.1.3 Similarities to Other Forms of Financing

The extent to which Project Finance should be regarded as a distinct wholesale banking product, or as a financing technique which incorporates a number of disciplines, is debatable. As a method of debt finance, project financing shares a number of the techniques and approaches found in other areas of wholesale banking:

Table 1: Comparison of Project Finance versus other wholesale financing techniques

Form of financing	Parallels/commonalities	Key differences
Corporate Lending	• Dependent on available cash flows to service debt • Term loan structures used	• Under an (unsecured) corporate loan, the lenders have recourse to all the assets of the company itself or in the case of a secured loan, a specific asset of the company • In Project Finance, the borrower is an SPV and the principle Lender security is are the future cashflows of the project itself – it is 'cashflow lending'
Securitisation (Asset Backed Securities)	• The borrower is an SPV • A form of 'off balance sheet' financing for the originator • The SPV issues bonds to fund	• A securitisation can only occur for cash generative assets. Project

Leveraged Buy-Out (LBO)	• Highly leveraged transactions	• In a project financing, the shareholders to the transaction are not contractually at risk if the project vehicle (borrower) defaults on its loans
Venture Capital	• Discrete number of equity investors • High focus on equity return of an investment	• Venture Capital investments are speculative assessments of a company's potential to generate returns.

4.1.4 Transactional Stakeholders

The sophisticated contracting arrangements of a project financing are underpinned by a detailed allocation of risks between a number of 'project stakeholders'.

Table provides a generic overview of the principle parties which typically feature in most project financings. An example of the typical contractual relationship between these parties is given in table below:

Table: Typical stakeholders of a Project Finance transaction

Stakeholder	Summary of role in a project financing
Sponsors	The equity investor(s) and owner(s) of the Project Company – can be a single party, or more frequently, a consortium of Sponsors Subsidiaries of the Sponsors may also act as sub-contractors, feedstock providers, or off-taker to the Project Company In PPP projects, the Government/Procurer may

	also retain an ownership stake in the project and therefore also be a Sponsor.
Procurement	Only relevant for PPP - the Procurer will be the municipality, and department of state responsible for tendering the project to the private sector, running the tender competition, evaluating the proposals, and selecting the preferred Sponsor consortium to implement the project.
Government	The government may contractually provide several undertakings to the Project Company, Sponsors, or Lenders which may include credit support in respect of the Procurer's payment obligations under a concession agreement.
Contractors	The substantive performance obligations of the Project Company to construct and operate the project will usually be done through engineering procurement and construction (EPC) and operations and maintenance (O&M) contracts respectively
Feedstock provider(s) and/or Offtaker	More typically found in utility, industrial, oil & gas, and petrochemical projects. One or more parties will be contractually obligated to provide feedstock to the project in return for payment. One or more parties will be contractually obligated to 'offtake' (purchase) some or all of the product or service produced by the project. Feedstock/Offtake contracts arc typically a key area of lender due diligence given their criticality to the overall economics of the project.

Lenders	Typically including one or more commercial banks and/or multilateral agencies and/or export credit agencies and/or bondholders

In addition to the core project stakeholders listed above, there are typically a host of other advisors, experts, and professionals who are either directly or indirectly involved in a project financing, including:

- Due diligence advisors to the Lenders which at a minimum will include technical and legal advisors but potentially also financial, insurance, auditing, tax, accounting, market, and environmental advisors (depending on the specifics of the project);

- Advisors to the Sponsors - typically financial, legal, and technical advisors at a minimum; and

- Under a PPP framework, advisors to the procuring authority/government – again, typically financial, legal, and technical advisors.

4.2 Project Cost Estimation & Working Capital Requirements

Project cost estimation and working capital requirements are crucial aspects of project planning and financial management. Let's delve into each of these components:

4.2.1 Project Cost Estimation:

Project cost estimation involves forecasting the expenses associated with initiating, executing, and completing a project. It encompasses various elements, including:

- ***Direct Costs:*** These are expenses directly attributable to the project, such as labor, materials, equipment, and subcontractor fees. Direct costs are typically quantifiable and allocated to specific project tasks or activities.

- ***Indirect Costs:*** Also known as overhead costs, these are expenses incurred to support the project but cannot be directly attributed to specific tasks. Examples include administrative expenses, utilities, rent, and insurance.

- ***Contingency Allowance:*** A contingency allowance is included in the project cost estimate to account for unforeseen events or risks that may impact project costs. Contingency funds provide a buffer to cover unexpected expenses or changes in project scope.

- ***Risk Management Costs:*** These include expenses related to identifying, assessing, and mitigating project risks. Costs associated with risk management activities, such as insurance premiums, risk assessments, and risk mitigation measures, are factored into the project cost estimate.

- ***Escalation and Inflation:*** Project cost estimates may account for escalation and inflation factors to account for anticipated increases in costs over time. These factors consider inflation rates, changes in market conditions, and cost trends for specific resources or materials.

- ***Professional Fees:*** Costs associated with hiring consultants, advisors, or project management services may be included in the project cost estimate. These fees cover specialized expertise and services required to plan, manage, and execute the project successfully.

4.2.2 Working Capital Requirements

Working capital refers to the funds needed to cover day-to-day operational expenses and support ongoing business activities. For a project, working capital requirements are essential to ensure smooth project execution and address short-term financing needs. Key considerations for working capital requirements include:

- ***Inventory and Materials:*** Projects may require an inventory of materials, supplies, or equipment to support project activities.

Working capital is needed to purchase, store, and manage inventory effectively throughout the project lifecycle.

- ***Labor Costs:*** Working capital is needed to cover labor costs, including wages, salaries, benefits, and payroll taxes for project personnel. Timely payment of wages and benefits ensures a motivated workforce and smooth project operations.

- ***Accounts Payable and Receivable:*** Projects may involve accounts payable for purchases of goods and services from suppliers and subcontractors. Working capital is needed to meet payment obligations and maintain positive supplier relationships. Likewise, accounts receivable may generate cash inflows from customer payments, which contribute to working capital.

- ***Operating Expenses:*** Working capital is required to cover various operating expenses, such as utilities, rent, insurance, and administrative costs. These expenses are necessary to support ongoing project activities and maintain business operations.

- ***Cash Reserves:*** Maintaining adequate cash reserves is essential to address unexpected expenses, emergencies, or fluctuations in cash flows. Working capital reserves provide a cushion to cover short-term funding gaps and ensure financial stability during project execution.

4.3 Sources of Funds

In project finance, funding is typically secured from various sources to finance large-scale projects. Here are some common sources of funds in project finance:

4.3.1 Equity Financing

- Equity financing involves raising funds by issuing shares or ownership stakes in the project to investors, such as individuals, institutional investors, or venture capital firms.

- Equity investors provide capital in exchange for ownership interests in the project and share in the project's profits and losses.

- Equity financing provides long-term funding and enhances the project's financial stability by reducing debt obligations.

4.3.2 Debt Financing

- Debt financing involves borrowing funds from lenders, such as banks, financial institutions, or bondholders, with the promise of repayment over time, typically with interest.

- Debt financing allows projects to leverage their assets and cash flows to access additional capital beyond their equity investment.

- Common forms of debt financing in project finance include bank loans, bonds, and other debt instruments tailored to the specific needs of the project.

4.3.3 Project-Specific Financing

- Project-specific financing involves raising funds through specialized financing mechanisms designed for the project's unique characteristics and requirements.

- Examples of project-specific financing include export credit agencies (ECAs), multilateral development banks (MDBs), and development finance institutions (DFIs) that provide financing for infrastructure and development projects in emerging markets.

4.3.4 Government Grants and Subsidies

- Government grants and subsidies may be available to support specific types of projects, such as renewable energy, infrastructure development, or research and development initiatives.

- Governments may provide financial incentives, tax credits, or direct grants to encourage investment in priority sectors and promote economic development.

4.3.5 Supplier and Vendor Financing

- Supplier and vendor financing involves obtaining financing directly from suppliers or vendors of goods and services used in the project.

- Suppliers may offer trade credit or financing arrangements to facilitate purchases and support project implementation, such as extended payment terms or installment payments.

4.3.6 Joint Ventures and Partnerships

- Joint ventures and partnerships involve collaborating with other companies or investors to pool resources and share risks and rewards.

- Joint venture partners contribute capital, expertise, and resources to the project in exchange for a share of ownership and profits.

4.3.7 Public-Private Partnerships (PPPs)

- Public-private partnerships involve collaboration between public-sector entities, such as governments or municipalities, and private-sector companies to finance, develop, and operate infrastructure projects.

- PPPs combine public funding, private investment, and operational expertise to deliver essential public services and infrastructure projects.

4.3.8 Crowdfunding and Peer-to-Peer Lending

- Crowdfunding platforms and peer-to-peer lending networks provide alternative sources of funding for projects, allowing individuals to invest directly in projects or lend money to project sponsors.

- Crowdfunding platforms enable project sponsors to raise capital from a large number of individual investors, often through online platforms and social media channels.

4.4 Capital Budgeting in Project Finance

Capital budgeting in project finance refers to the process of evaluating and selecting investment projects based on their potential to generate returns and create value for the organization. It involves analyzing and comparing the costs and benefits of different investment opportunities to determine which projects are worth pursuing. Here are the key components of capital budgeting in project finance:

4.4.1 Project Identification and Screening:

- The first step in capital budgeting is to identify potential investment projects that align with the organization's strategic objectives and investment criteria.

- Projects are screened based on their feasibility, relevance, and alignment with the organization's goals and risk appetite.

4.4.2 Project Evaluation and Analysis:

- Once potential projects are identified, they undergo a thorough evaluation and analysis to assess their financial viability and potential returns.

- Project analysis involves estimating the project's cash flows, including initial investment costs, operating cash flows, and terminal cash flows.

- Techniques such as net present value (NPV), internal rate of return (IRR), payback period, and profitability index are used to evaluate the financial attractiveness of investment projects.

4.4.3 Cost Estimation and Budgeting:

- Capital budgeting requires estimating the costs associated with each investment project, including initial capital expenditures, operating expenses, maintenance costs, and financing costs.

- Accurate cost estimation is essential for determining the project's total investment outlay and evaluating its financial feasibility.

4.4.4 Cash Flow Forecasting:

- Cash flow forecasting involves projecting the cash inflows and outflows associated with the investment project over its expected life cycle.

- Cash flow projections consider factors such as revenue generation, operating expenses, taxes, depreciation, and working capital requirements.

- Forecasted cash flows are discounted to their present value using an appropriate discount rate to determine the project's net present value (NPV) and internal rate of return (IRR).

4.4.5. Risk Assessment and Sensitivity Analysis:

- Capital budgeting involves assessing the risks and uncertainties associated with investment projects and conducting sensitivity analysis to evaluate their impact on project outcomes.

- Risks such as market volatility, regulatory changes, technological obsolescence, and project-specific risks are identified and analyzed to determine their potential impact on project profitability.

- Sensitivity analysis evaluates how changes in key variables, such as revenue projections, cost estimates, and discount rates, affect the project's financial performance and investment decisions.

4.4.6 Investment Decision Making:

- Based on the evaluation and analysis of investment projects, investment decisions are made to determine which projects to pursue, defer, or reject.

- Projects with positive NPV, higher IRR, and shorter payback periods are typically prioritized, as they indicate higher returns and faster recovery of investment capital.

- Investment decisions consider factors such as strategic alignment, risk profile, capital constraints, and available investment opportunities.

4.4.7 Post-Investment Evaluation and Monitoring:

- After investment decisions are made, ongoing monitoring and evaluation of investment projects are essential to track their performance and ensure they deliver the expected returns.

- Post-investment evaluation involves comparing actual project performance against projected outcomes, identifying variances, and implementing corrective actions as needed.

- Continuous monitoring helps identify emerging risks, opportunities for optimization, and lessons learned for future capital budgeting decisions.

4.5 Risk & Uncertainty in Project Evaluation

Risk and uncertainty are inherent in project evaluation and play a significant role in assessing the feasibility and potential outcomes of investment projects. Here's how risk and uncertainty impact project evaluation:

4.5.1. Risk in Project Evaluation

Risk refers to the possibility of adverse outcomes or deviations from expected results that may impact the success of a project. Risks can arise from various sources, including market conditions, technology, regulatory changes, project execution, and external factors. In project evaluation:

- ***Risk Identification:*** The first step is to identify and analyze potential risks that may affect the project's objectives, timeline, budget, and outcomes. This involves assessing both internal and external risks that could impact project performance.

- ***Risk Assessment:*** Once risks are identified, they are assessed in terms of their likelihood of occurrence and potential impact on the project. Risks with higher probability and severity are prioritized for further analysis and mitigation.

- ***Risk Mitigation:*** Risk mitigation strategies are developed to manage and reduce the impact of identified risks on the project. This may include implementing risk management plans, contingency measures, insurance, hedging strategies, or contractual arrangements to transfer or mitigate risks.

- **Risk Monitoring and Control:** Throughout the project lifecycle, risks are monitored and controlled to track their evolution, assess their impact on project performance, and implement timely corrective actions. Continuous risk management helps minimize the likelihood and severity of adverse outcomes.

4.5.2. Uncertainty in Project Evaluation:

Uncertainty refers to the lack of knowledge or predictability regarding future events or outcomes, making it challenging to assess their likelihood or impact. Uncertainty arises from factors such as market dynamics, technological changes, regulatory uncertainty, and incomplete information. In project evaluation:

- ***Scenario Analysis:*** Given the uncertainty surrounding future events, scenario analysis involves evaluating different possible scenarios or outcomes based on various assumptions and factors. This helps assess the range of potential outcomes and their associated risks and opportunities.

- ***Sensitivity Analysis:*** Sensitivity analysis assesses how changes in key variables or assumptions affect project outcomes, such as revenue projections, cost estimates, or discount rates. By varying input parameters, sensitivity analysis identifies the most critical drivers of project performance and their impact on financial metrics.

- ***Monte Carlo Simulation:*** Monte Carlo simulation is a probabilistic technique used to model and analyze the impact of uncertainty on project outcomes. By simulating thousands of possible scenarios based on probability distributions of input variables, Monte Carlo simulation provides a probabilistic assessment of project risks and uncertainties.

- ***Flexibility and Adaptability:*** In the face of uncertainty, projects must be designed to be flexible and adaptable to changing conditions or unforeseen events. This may involve incorporating flexibility into project plans, contracts, and decision-making processes to respond effectively to evolving circumstances.

4.5.3. Integration of Risk and Uncertainty in Project Evaluation:

Effective project evaluation considers both risk and uncertainty to make informed decisions and mitigate potential adverse impacts. By systematically assessing risks, analyzing uncertainties, and incorporating risk management strategies, project evaluations can provide a more realistic assessment of project feasibility, optimize resource allocation, and enhance project outcomes.

4.6 Preparation of Projected Financial Statements

Preparing projected financial statements involves forecasting the future financial performance and position of a business or project based on assumptions and expectations. Here's a step-by-step guide to preparing projected financial statements:

4.6.1. Gather Historical Data

Start by gathering historical financial data for the business or project, including income statements, balance sheets, and cash flow statements for previous periods. This data serves as a baseline for projecting future financial performance.

4.6.2. Define Assumptions

Identify and document the assumptions that will drive the projections. Assumptions may include factors such as sales growth rates, cost of goods sold (COGS), operating expenses, capital expenditures, financing costs, and tax rates. Assumptions should be based on thorough analysis and consideration of market trends, industry benchmarks, and business strategies.

4.6.3. Project Revenue

Forecast revenues for the projected period based on expected sales volumes, pricing strategies, and market demand. Consider factors such as market trends, customer preferences, competitive landscape, and potential growth opportunities.

Break down revenue projections by product/service categories, customer segments, geographic regions, or other relevant factors to provide detailed insights into revenue sources.

4.6.4. Estimate Cost of Goods Sold (COGS)

Estimate the cost of goods sold (COGS) or cost of sales associated with producing or delivering the projected revenue. This includes direct costs such as materials, labor, and overhead expenses directly attributable to the production or delivery of goods/services.

Use historical cost data, industry benchmarks, and anticipated changes in input costs to estimate COGS accurately.

4.6.5. Project Operating Expenses

Forecast operating expenses for the projected period, including salaries, wages, rent, utilities, marketing expenses, administrative costs, and other overhead expenses. Consider historical spending patterns, planned investments, cost-saving initiatives, and other factors that may impact operating expenses.

4.6.6. Calculate Depreciation and Amortization

Estimate depreciation and amortization expenses for the projected period based on the expected useful life of assets and applicable accounting methods. Consider planned capital expenditures, asset acquisitions, and disposals when estimating depreciation and amortization.

4.6.7. Estimate Other Income and Expenses

Project other income and expenses, such as interest income, interest expenses, dividends, gains/losses on investments, and non-operating income/expenses.

Consider the impact of financing activities, investments, and other non-operating transactions on the projected financial statements.

4.6.8. Calculate Taxes

Estimate taxes payable for the projected period based on applicable tax rates, tax laws, and tax planning strategies.

Consider tax deductions, credits, and incentives available to the business/project when calculating taxes payable.

4.6.9. Prepare Projected Income Statement

Use the projected revenue, COGS, operating expenses, depreciation, amortization, other income/expenses, and taxes to prepare the projected income statement (also known as the profit and loss statement).

Present the projected income statement in a format that highlights key revenue and expense categories and calculates net income/loss for the projected period.

4.6.10. Project Cash Flows

Forecast cash inflows and outflows for the projected period based on the projected income statement, changes in working capital, capital expenditures, financing activities, and other relevant factors.

Prepare the projected cash flow statement to show cash flows from operating activities, investing activities, financing activities, and the net change in cash and cash equivalents.

4.6.11. Prepare Projected Balance Sheet

Use the projected cash flows, asset purchases, debt repayments, equity issuances, and other transactions to prepare the projected balance sheet.

Present the projected balance sheet in a format that shows assets, liabilities, and shareholders' equity at the end of the projected period.

4.6.12. Review and Validate Projections

Review the projected financial statements to ensure accuracy, consistency, and alignment with the underlying assumptions and expectations.

Validate the projections by comparing them to historical data, industry benchmarks, market research, and other relevant sources of information.

Conduct sensitivity analysis to assess the impact of changes in key assumptions on the projected financial statements and evaluate the robustness of the projections.

4.6.13. Document Assumptions and Methodology

Document the assumptions, methodologies, and sources of information used to prepare the projected financial statements.

Provide explanations and justifications for key assumptions and decisions made during the projection process to enhance transparency and credibility.

4.6.14. Present Projected Financial Statements

Present the projected financial statements in a clear, concise, and understandable format suitable for internal review, stakeholder communication, and decision-making purposes.

Highlight key assumptions, trends, risks, and opportunities reflected in the projected financial statements to facilitate understanding and interpretation.

4.6.15. Update and Monitor Projections

Regularly update and monitor the projected financial statements to reflect changes in business conditions, market dynamics, and other factors affecting the project.

Review actual performance against projected results, identify variances, and adjust projections as needed to maintain accuracy and relevance.

4.7 Projected Balance Sheet

A projected balance sheet provides an estimate of a company's financial position at a specific point in the future. It includes assets, liabilities, and shareholders' equity, projected based on assumptions and expectations about future business operations and financial performance. Here's how to prepare a projected balance sheet:

1. **Gather Historical Data:** Start by gathering historical balance sheets for the company for reference. This will provide a baseline for projecting future balances.

2. **Define Assumptions:** Identify and document the assumptions that will drive the projections. Assumptions may include factors such as sales growth rates, cost structures, capital expenditures, financing activities, and other relevant variables.

3. **Project Assets:** Estimate the value of current assets, including cash and cash equivalents, accounts receivable, inventory, and prepaid expenses. Use historical trends, growth projections, and other factors to estimate future values. Project long-term assets, such as property, plant, and equipment (PP&E), intangible assets, and investments. Consider planned capital expenditures, asset purchases, depreciation, and amortization.

4. **Project Liabilities:** Estimate current liabilities, including accounts payable, accrued expenses, short-term debt, and current portions of long-term debt. Use historical data and expected changes in

business operations to forecast future liabilities. Project long-term liabilities, such as long-term debt, leases, and deferred tax liabilities. Consider planned financing activities, debt repayments, and other obligations.

5. ***Calculate Shareholders' Equity:*** Estimate shareholders' equity by subtracting total liabilities from total assets. Shareholders' equity represents the residual value of assets after deducting liabilities and reflects the owners' claims on the company's assets. Consider changes in equity, such as stock issuances, repurchases, dividends, and retained earnings. Factor in expected changes in the company's capital structure and financing activities.

6. ***Prepare the Projected Balance Sheet:*** Organize the projected balance sheet into three main sections: assets, liabilities, and shareholders' equity. List current assets first, followed by long-term assets. Similarly, list current liabilities first, followed by long-term liabilities. Present shareholders' equity as the final section, calculated as the residual value after deducting liabilities from assets. Use clear formatting and labels to ensure the balance sheet is easy to read and understand.

7. ***Review and Validate Projections:*** Review the projected balance sheet to ensure accuracy, consistency, and alignment with the underlying assumptions and expectations. Validate the projections by comparing them to historical data, industry benchmarks, market research, and other relevant sources of information. Conduct sensitivity analysis to assess the impact of changes in key assumptions on the projected balance sheet and evaluate the robustness of the projections.

8. ***Document Assumptions and Methodology:*** Document the assumptions, methodologies, and sources of information used to prepare the projected balance sheet. Provide explanations and justifications for key assumptions and decisions made during the projection process to enhance transparency and credibility.

9. ***Present the Projected Balance Sheet:*** Present the projected balance sheet in a clear, concise, and understandable format suitable for internal review, stakeholder communication, and decision-making purposes. Highlight key assumptions, trends, risks, and opportunities reflected in the projected balance sheet to facilitate understanding and interpretation.

10. ***Update and Monitor Projections:*** Regularly update and monitor the projected balance sheet to reflect changes in business conditions, market dynamics, and other factors affecting the company. Review actual performance against projected results, identify variances, and adjust projections as needed to maintain accuracy and relevance.

4.8 Projected Income Statement

A projected income statement shows an estimate of the profits and losses in a future period – the next quarter or the next fiscal year, for instance. It uses the same format as a regular income statement but projects the future rather than recording numbers from the past. In this blog post, we will cover how to use an income statement template to understand what a project income statement is and how it works.

Revenues	$XXXX
Cost of Goods Sold	(XXXX)
Gross Profit	$XXXX
Operating Expenses	
Commissions	(XXXX)
Marketing Expenses	(XXXX)
Office Expenses	(XXXX)
Total Operating Expenses	($XXXX)
Net Income	$XXXX

You start at the top with the total amount of sales revenue made during the accounting period. Then you go down, one step at a time. At each step, you make a deduction for certain costs or other operating expenses associated with earning revenue, which brings you to a specific subtotal. At the bottom of the stairs, after deducting all expenses, you learn how much you earned or lost during the accounting period. People often call this "the bottom line."

4.8.1 Components of Income Statement Template

A typical income statement for a small business will include the following steps, though they are not limited to using only these three:

1. Gross Profit

2. Operating Income

3. Net Income

4.8.1.1 *Gross Profit*

Generally the first major subtotal on an income statement, Gross Profit is calculated by deducting Cost of Goods Sold from Revenues.

Gross Profit = Revenues - Cost of Goods Sold

4.8.1.2 *Operating Income*

Following the Income Statement Template, the next major subtotal, Operating Income, is calculated by deducting Fixed Expenses (also known as Operating Expenses) from Gross Profit.

Operating Expenses include costs such as the salaries of any employee personnel, as well as any research and development costs, marketing costs, and more. These are considered operating expenses because, unlike the costs included in the Costs of Goods Sold, they cannot be directly linked to the production of products or services being sold.

We also deduct depreciation from Gross Profit to determine Operating Income. Depreciation takes into account the wear and tear on assets, such as machinery, tools, and furniture that are used over the long term. Companies spread the cost of these assets over the periods they are used. This process of spreading these costs is called depreciation or amortization. The "charge" for using these assets during the period is a fraction of the original cost of the assets.

Operating Income = Gross Profit - Fixed Expenses

4.8.1.3 Net Income

Though larger companies may have additional subtotals or steps on their income statements after the calculation of Operating Income, much of this is outside the scope of our discussions.

After we have determined Operating Income, the last thing we need to do before determining the final subtotal, Net Income, is figure out our income tax expense. Though income tax expense varies widely depending on how a business is structured, it can generally be estimated using publicly available tax brackets. Once income tax expense has been deducted from Operating Income, we are left with the "bottom line" figure of Net Income, or Net Loss if the number is negative. This figure tells us how much a company has earned or lost during an accounting period.

Net Income = Gross Profit - Operating Income

4.8.2 Projected Income Statement Walkthrough Using Income Statement Template

Let's say you are a small business owner and are considering an expansion into the widgets business. You have decided to put together a projected income statement for the following year to see if the new product is worthwhile.

Revenue

The first item you need to estimate is your revenue, also known as sales to customers.

You estimate that you can sell 1,000 widgets at an average price of $50 each, so your revenue estimate is $50,000.

Cost of Goods Sold

Next, you need to estimate your cost of goods sold. This is the cost of buying or producing the widgets.

In this case, you have already located a supplier who will sell them to you at $1,500 for 100 widgets, or $15 each. So, your estimated cost of goods sold for the 1,000 widgets you anticipate selling will be 1,000 * $15 = $15,000.

Since Gross Profit is simply Revenue - Cost of Goods Sold, in this example, the Gross Profit is $50,000 - $15,000 = $35,000.

Next, you need to estimate the additional operating costs you'll incur by offering this product. You'll need to pay a salesperson a 10% commission on sales of your widgets, which is $5 each. For the 1,000 anticipated sales, this will be $5,000 for the year.

You also anticipate spending $500 a month for brochures and $1,500 a month for additional office costs, such as office supplies, telephone calls, and other odds and ends. Operating expenses are generally shown in broad categories, so your operating expense projection will be:

Commissions: $5,000

Marketing costs: $6,000 ($500 a month * 12 months)

Office costs: $18,000 ($1,500 a month * 12 months)

Total: $29,000

Net Income

Finally, we can estimate our net income to fill the last section of the income statement template.

Reminder: Net Income = Gross Profit - Operating Income

Net income is our gross profit of $35,000 minus our operating expenses of $29,000 = $6,000 for the year.

The Final Projection

Now that you've put together the revenues and costs of this venture, it's time to create your projected income statement. Here is the final projection, in standard income statement template format:

XYZ Company

Projected Income Statement

For the Year Ended December 31, 20XX

Revenues	$50,000
Cost of Goods Sold	(15,000)
Gross Profit	$35,000
Operating Expenses	
Commissions	(5,000)
Marketing Expenses	(6,000)
Office Expenses	(18,000)
Total Operating Expenses	($29,000)
Net Income	$6,000

4.9 Projected Funds & Cash Flow Statements

A cash flow projection statement is a financial record that both records a company's current cash flow and estimates cash flow in the future. This includes predicting the income it might receive in the coming months and the expenses it incurs. Cash flow is the amount of money a company earns and spends, and it typically records this in its cash flow statement. Here's some information to include in this statement:

- Starting balance

- Incoming cash

- Outgoing expenses

- Total cash and expenses

- Total predicted cash flow

- Ending balance

- Pay period

4.9.1 Benefits of Cash Flow Projection Statements

There are several key reasons you may create a projected cash flow statement, including:

Prepare for potential shortages: Estimating a company's future cash flow can help you identify any months where it might have a negative cash flow. Consider investigating where you might be able to lower the company's expenses during that time or increase cash flow during other months.

Plan for surpluses: With this statement, you can also identify what months a company may expect a surplus of cash. Based on that information, you might invest in new equipment or marketing or provide bonuses for the company's staff.

Make future estimates accurately: By projecting across periods, you can compare this data to the actual figures from last year. This may help you identify trends and see how you might consider increasing costs, like for building materials.

Anticipate change: If the company experiences a big change, such as securing a new office space or hiring a new employee, you likely want to project cash flow. This helps determine if it's necessary to increase sales to maintain a positive cash flow or make other adjustments to the company's finances.

Increase credibility: You might use a cash flow projection statement to show investors or loan providers the company's estimated cash flow. This might improve your chances of getting approved, increasing the company's credibility as a borrower.

Adjust early: Creating a projection statement allows you to make adjustments early. For example, you might negotiate lower interest rates, purchase cheaper equipment, or increase marketing efforts depending on whether the company's cash flow is positive or negative.

4.9.2 How to create a cash flow projection statement

There are several steps you can take to create a cash flow projection statement:

4.9.2.1. Calculate the current cash amount

The first figure to calculate is the total cash the company has. If you create your projections at the end of the month, calculate how much cash the company earned and subtract the amount of cash the company spent to get this figure. At the top of the company's statement, you can include this number as the "opening amount," which shows how much cash the company starts with for the following month.

4.9.2.2. Estimate projected cash

The next component of your statement is a projection of the cash the company expects to earn. This serves as your cash-in figure. Create a line item for each possible cash source, including:

Cash earned from operating activities

This refers to money generated from the company's operations. You can calculate cash flow from operations using either the direct or indirect method. The direct method involves taking all the company's cash collections from operations and subtracting all its cash disbursements from operations. The indirect method requires you to start with net income from the company's income statement and make adjustments to undo the effect of the accruals made during the reporting period.

Cash flow from investing activities

This refers to cash flows related to the selling and buying of long-term assets. These assets may include equipment, facilities, and property. It's important to remember that this only includes investing activities involving free cash, not debt.

This refers to cash outflows and inflows related to financing activities, such as cash flows from both equity and debt financing, which is cash flows from raising cash and paying back debts to creditors and investors. When using generally accepted accounting principles (GAAP), cash flow from financing activities also includes dividends paid. This may appear in the operating section when using the International Financial Reporting Standards (IFRS).

4.9.2.3. Estimate potential expenses

Similar to your cash-in section, calculating the company's expenses is important to ensure you plan to earn more than you spend. This can include both regular expenses like rent and utilities and any one-time costs the company might incur in certain months, like annual charges. For some variable expenses, such as the cost of goods, estimate these amounts based on what you expect them to cost.

Once you have your projected cash and expenses, you can calculate the company's projected cash flow using the following equation: Projected cash flow = total projected cash - total projected expenses. The total project cash is incoming, and the total project expenses are outgoing. The projected cash flow figure could be positive or negative, depending on which of the incoming or outgoing cash amounts are higher. You can use this figure to create the next period's opening balance.

4.9.2.5. Add the projected cash flow figure to the current cash amount

If the company's cash flow is positive, add this number to your opening balance to calculate the next month's opening figure. If it's negative, subtract the cash flow amount. This figure can help you identify if the company earns enough money during future pay periods to cover its expenses and make a profit. If you're calculating monthly, this figure can be the opening cash amount for the following month.

Cash flow projection statement example

Here's an example of a cash flow projection scenario and statement: Sophia wants to create a cash flow projection for the second half of the year to ensure she has enough cash to cover her expenses and still earn a profit. At the end of June, her business has $10,000 in cash. She creates a projected cash flow statement with all her projected income and expenses for July through December:

	July	August	September	October	November	December
Starting balance	$10,000	$14,400	$13,100	$14,200	$13,400	$13,400
Incoming cash						
Sales	$5,000	$2,000	$3,000	$1,000	$1,000	$4,000
Credit payments	$1,000	$0	$500	$0	$500	$500
Total incoming	$6,000	$2,000	$3,500	$1,000	$1,500	$4,500
Outgoing cash						
Rent	$1,000	$1,000	$1,000	$1,000	$1,000	$1,000
Utilities	$400	$500	$400	$400	$400	$800
Marketing	$200	$800	$1,000	$400	$100	$400
Total outgoing						
Cash flow	$4,400	($300)	$1,100	($800)	$0	$4,300
Ending	$14,400	$13,100	$14,200	$13,400	$13,400	$18,700

	July	August	September	October	November	December
balance						

Sophia's projected cash flow for the second half of the year is $8,700. Using these projections, she might calculate some additional investments she can make to increase her cash flow.

4.10 Preparation of Detailed Project Report

Detailed Project Reports (DPRs) are the outputs of the planning and design phase of a project. DPR is a very detailed and elaborate plan for a project indicating the overall program, different roles and responsibilities, activities, and resources required for the project. To be more precise,

A DPR is a final, detailed appraisal report on the project and a blueprint for its execution and eventual operation. It provides details of the basic program the roles and responsibilities, all the activities to be carried out the resources required, and possible risks with recommended measures to counter them.

The success of the project is measured based on:

- Whether the project was completed on time.

- Whether the actual cost of the project was within reasonable limits of escalation.

- Whether after completion of the project, it was able to deliver the products of desired quality and in adequate quantity to clients' satisfaction at profitable costs.

- Whether the project gestation period was within the planned duration.

The design stage is a blueprint that on paper gives a great length and detail of what has to be done to convert the corporate investment into a feasible project idea and ultimately a profit making enterprise.

The top management policy guidelines, their impact on the project life, appraisal in terms of financial viability are dealt in great detail. The DPR is the basic of specification, contract drawings, detailed technical feasibility, financial feasibility, execution of project from practical point of view. The DPR should also highlight the nature of inherent risks in the project & potential external risks that will influence the outcome of the project. Also, the DPR should give the measures for risk management and risk mitigation.

The main sub-division in a DPR is:

- General Information of the project.

- Background and the experience of the project promoters.

- Details and working results of industrial concerns already owned and promoted by the project promoters.

- Details of the proposed project:

    1. Plant capacity

    2. Manufacturing procedure adopted

    3. Technical know-how/ tie-ups.

    4. Management teams for the project.

    5. Details of land, buildings plants, and machinery.

    6. Details of infrastructural facilities (power, water supply, transport facilities, etc.)

    7. Raw material requirement/ availability.

    8. Effluents produced by the project & treatment procedures adopted.

    9. Labor requirement and availability.

- Schedule of implementation of the project.

- Project cost.

- Means of financial projects.

- Working capital requirement/arrangements made.

- Marketing and selling arrangements made.

- Profitability and cash flow estimates.

- Mode of repayment of loans.

- Government approvals. Local body consents and statutory permissions.

- Details of collateral security that can be offered to the financial institutions.

4.10.1 Preparation of DPR

The preparation of DPR requires a wide variety of expertise. Several decisions are mutually related. For example: the requirement and training plan are dependent on the nature of the technology, availability in the general employment market in the region, need for foreign collaboration and training, the extent of specialized plant and equipment supplied from abroad, etc.

Financial requirements are dependent on the schedule for the implementation of the project. The nature of the issue to be included in the commercial terms and conditions depends on the extent of the spread of the contractors. If only local and regional parties are in the picture, the scope and jurisdiction for disputes will be restricted.

Several issues largely depend upon managerial perceptions and top management policies. On the whole preparation of DPR is a complete task. Therefore highly specialized agencies have come up in different areas, that undertake such tasks for clients.

They are usually known as technical consultancy organizations. They specialize in some particular field. For example, Dastur & co specializes in metallurgical industries, and Engineers India Ltd. specializes in oil sectors.

Even for medium-sized projects, a capable consulting firm must be entrusted with the task of formulating the DPR.

4.10.2 Steps of Preparation of DPR

- The client interacts with a consultant.

- The consultant takes all required inputs from the client & does necessary first-phase studies.

- The client evaluates it & makes all necessary changes & requests a consultant to do the necessary modifications.

- The consultant submits the revised draft for approval.

- The consultant submits the final DPR after getting approval from the client.

4.10.3 Evaluation of DPR

The final responsibility of the project lies with the owners. Therefore, the owner's organization must have an appropriate mechanism for project evaluation of a DPR submitted by the consultant. Apart from care in selecting the most suitable consultant in the first place, the owners must pose the following questions.

- What are the sources of critical data & information that have formed the basic premises of the DPR, like demand, capital cost, input cost, etc.?

- The extent to which the strategic plan of top management has been reflected in the design and the repair?

- What were the various alternatives considered, and the methodology followed for choosing one among them?

- The extent to which the design fulfills all applicable statutory requirements and regulations, both currently in force and those that may be foreseen?

- Identification of potential problems, bottlenecks, and/or major risks involved in the project.

- Degree of detailing.

- Influence of complementary/ completing projects.

- Scope for future expansion/modification/adaptation to new technologies and so on.

The above list is a sample of the types of questions that the owners may pose to the consultant during the process of selection, appraisal of the first draft, and before approval.

4.10.4 Location of the Project

One of the important issues related to project decisions and DPR preparation is the location of the project. The location of project can be:

- Input or supply oriented

- Output or market-oriented.

Input or supply-oriented: The major consideration governing the location decision concerns the availability of various inputs for the project & their transportation from respective sources to the project site. Whenever a project entails the processing of bulky raw materials and the processing reduces the bulk by refining/processing operation, it makes economic sense to move the project nearer the supplies to cut down the transportation costs. The strategy of NTPC to locate major pit-head thermal power plants stems from this logic. Instead of transporting coal over long distances, it may be more economical to convert coal into electrical energy at the pit head itself and transmit the electrical energy into a high-voltage transmission system to consumption centres. With the advent of high voltage direct current transmission technology, such options have become more cost-effective.

Output or market oriented: The gas based power plants may be located near the consumption centres, particularly if gas pipelines have already been laid nearby for other projects. This enables saving on the transmission line costs and power losses in transmission.

The location strategy is largely governed by total transportation cost for entire chain, including transportation of all inputs of various sources to the processing site and that of all outputs to the consumption centres. This exercise needs the sources and quantities of all the supplies available , their unit transportation cost to each location and the demands at different consumption centres, coupled with the unit transportation cost to the finished goods to each consumption centre of each location.

The location strategy also depends on:

- The regulatory framework of thr region.

- Availability of skilled/unskilled manpower

- Industrial relations situation.

- Infrastructural support.

4.10.5 Layout of the project

The layout itself has profound implication on the profitability and efficiency of any enterprises. Even safety considerations can lead to major changes in the layout.

The layout for a project determines the location of various departments, processes; work centres, machines & service function as well as transportation routes for the movement of materials through these facilities.

A good layout should try to reduce material handling cost to the minimum, ensure flow of men and materials between processes without any back tracking, provide adequate safety for men and equipment and enhance Labor productivity & efficiency.

Safety must be a very important consideration for deciding locations of potentially hazardous facilities. For instance storage of hazardous &

inflammable chemicals & materials must be located far away from the general centre of activities at economical & practically feasible distance.

Facilities which are prone to fire hazards should be located in a fashion that is easy and quick for multiple fire tenders to arrive & extinguish the fire. It may be worthwhile to give a specific safety check to a layout before finalising it.

4.10.6 Equipment & Process Technology (EPT)

The equipment and process technology (EPT) decisions are related to design of facilities and system that produce and deliver goods, products and services of desired quality and required quantity. EPT are categorised as follows:

Output decisions are related to demand forecast and marketing strategy for achieving planned market share.

The input and process decisions are complementary to each other. The input and process decisions contribute significantly to "Make or Buy" type of decisions. The "Make or Buy" decisions lead to finalisation of various inputs as well as processing and assembly requirements.

Once the production processes are identified then next set of decisions are related to choice of technology. Choice of technology decisions has to be ajudicious mix of capital and Labor components which are the major factor of production.

Use of modern state of art technology ensures more automation, requiring less Labor but leads to high initial investment. On the contrary use of traditional technology and processes leads to lower automation with requirement of more Labor and lower initial investment.

Therefore, the trade-off lies between high capital and lower Labor cost on one hand and low capital and high Labor cost on the other hand.

Apart from cost considerations and relative proportion of mechanisation, other factors that are to be considered are scale of operations: quality and level of skills required also influence the choice of technology decisions.

Depending on the market share & capacity forecasts, a particular level of technology may be the optimum choice. In event of low market demand & lack of availability of skilled work force to operate high end & high volume technology may lead to sub optimal utilisation of the said technology.

Also, there would be substantial increase in the subsequent maintenance costs which may raised affordability issues. Thus, the choice of EPT is a complex task, requiring wide knowledge & information about different options with relative merits and demerits of each option.

In case the procurement of EPT requires high initial investment or decision making process is taking unusually long time then the option of technology collaboration may be explored.

In this option, the organisation may explore possibilities of technical collaboration agreement with some organisation that has had considerable experience in use of the proposed technology and are in position to impart their knowledge to others. Such a collaborating organisation may be found in the country or may be from abroad.

4.10.7 Environmental Impact Assessment (EIA)

EPT must have a dedicated section of environmental Impact Assessment (EIA). Such an assessment would have the specifications of the environment which is known as the base level specification before setting up a project.

Thereafter, an estimate should be made as to the impact of the project operations on various base level parameters. These could co0ver air, water and soil parameters. The disposal of soil, liquid and gaseous effluents generated by the project would lead to increase in pollution load over the base levels.

After estimating the impact of the project on the base level of the environment the DPR should recommend specific control measures & effluent treatment facilities so that the environment pollution can be controlled within permissible limits.

The DPR should ensure that the provisions are adequate for fulfilling the legal requirements in the locality where the project is scheduled to come up. This calls for the detailed knowledge of all the state level and national level provisions with respect to environmental protection.

Many of the provisions call for obtaining clearances from controlling bodies. The DPR should also include a time schedule for obtaining all the required clearances.

4.10.8 Commercial aspects

DPR is related to general guidelines and conditions that should govern all types of contractual relationships likely to be entered into during the project.

In particular, general guidelines for any eventual arbitration procedures are indicated, specifying the nature of issue that may be referred for arbitration, choice of arbitrator by both the parties and the place where such proceedings should be held.

DPR should also include guidelines related to supply, erection, and commissioning & guarantee test of various equipment's required for the project.

DPR should also lay guidelines for tendering process whether to follow single stage or two stage tendering. It may also contain model document and formats related to invitation to tenders, specifications etc.

DPR will also contain guidelines for vendor short-listing and networking. Some points related to vender detailing that are highlighted in the DPR are as cited below:

- Commitment with respect to delivery period & penalty conditions, in case of failure to fulfil the commitment.

- General terms of payment including progress payment.

- Inspection and testing procedure and customer hold points.

- Network plan for the contract and monitoring and control system.

- Guarantee test, schedule, procedure, criteria for success and accompanying bank guarantee.

- Responsibility for damage in transit or during erection and/ or commissioning.

- Condition of admissibility of any increase in the price of the contract.

- Contract variations and the manner of handling them.

- Mobilisation advance to be paid initially.

- Responsibility to supply the equipment's and necessary accessories and spare parts.

4.10.9 Financial Aspects

The DPR incorporates a much detailed projection of the costs and revenues expected during the projected lifespan of the operation phase. The principal input to this comes from operational costs.

Also the other financing cost like depreciation, interest on long term loans and short term working capital loans, writing off of pre-operative & preliminary expenses, guarantee commission etc. Income tax calculation are also included.

The DPR provides projections for the following statements:

- Profit and loss statement.

- The balance sheet.

- The fund flow statement.

For the project phase, the DPR provides an estimate of the phase requirement of capital. This plan forms the basis of a strategic plan for raising the funds from external sources like terms lending institutions and through public issue of stocks and/or bonds.

The DPR would include a recommendation schedule for ensuring adequate flow of funds for the timely completion of the project with adequate provision for normal contingencies.

The DPR would also include for the project phase a recommended system of monitoring & control of the financial progress of the project, vis-a-vis the physical progress. The system is an essential ingredient for adequate financial control during the execution & the termination phase of the project.

4.10.10 Socio-economic Aspects

Morden day projects also analyse the socio-economic impacts on their immediate surroundings. The attitude of local residents plays a crucial role in the successful completion of the project in any new locality or region.

Generally, any medium to large type of project will lead to displacement of original residents and tenants of the land & bring about a significant change in the pattern of earning livelihood, brings in wide disparity in the standards of living between those who are employed in the project and those who are left out of it, raises large employment expectations among the local population.

The effect are more glaring based on the size of investments, level of technology used & innovation potential of the project. However not all factors contribute in the socio-economic influence but it is for sure that a combination of factors based on the size & type of project will surely lead to creation of social discontent.

The project is seen as a source of social turmoil & discontent & its progress gets affected severally through different forms of social unrest. It is, therefore, essential to make an effort at the early stage in planning process to reach out the population likely to be affected by the project.

Community based & community participated demographic surveys may be conducted for identifying the options for direct as well as indirect source of employment. DPR should also highlight planning & execution methods of specific community development programmes which help in developing a symbiotic relationship with the local community.

4.11 Project Finance

The answer to 'What is project finance?' is that it is the funding of capital-intensive projects related to sectors such as manufacturing, energy, health care and mining. It involves the usage of the non-recourse financial structure where a sponsor has no obligation to pay back the lenders if the revenue generated by a project is insufficient to cover the principal amount and the interest. The lender can only sell a borrower's assets but cannot force them to pay more compensation if the value of all the assets does not cover the debt amount. Project financing involves multiple parties forming a corporation to start a large-scale project. First, they create a project company known as a special purpose vehicle (SPV), which is a subsidiary company. The subsidiary company isolates the risks associated with the parent company's assets or ventures. This ensures that the project company retains its legal status if the parent entities go bankrupt. Next, several lenders, such as equity stockholders, commercial banks and the government, finance the project. The project company uses this capital to fund its operations and pays back the loan from the cash flows it generates.

4.11.1 Project Financing Participants

Below is a list of participants in a large-scale project:

- ***Sponsor:*** Project sponsors are entities that form a partnership to create a project company. All entities that form a partnership have a set of obligations to an SPV.

- ***Equity investors:*** They provide capital to finance the project company's operations in return for partial ownership of the company in the form of shares. They do this in anticipation of a higher return over time based on a project's success.

- ***Construction contractor:*** A construction contractor signs an agreement to undertake the design and construction of a project.

- ***Operator:*** Operators can be multinational companies or joint ventures responsible for ensuring project asset quality. These may include properties and tangible or intangible assets.

- ***Feedstock supplier:*** Feedstock suppliers sign a long-term agreement to provide raw materials for processing or manufacturing products. The feedstock may include crude oil, gasoline, electricity and other raw materials.

- ***Lender:*** Lenders can be a single company or a group of companies that provide funds to a project company for its construction and development work. They hold the company's assets as collateral.

- ***Project off-taker:*** Off-takers are parties that sign an agreement to buy a part or all of a company's output.

4.11.2 Three Phases of Project Finance

The project financing process includes three phases, including:

4.11.2.1. Pre-financing stage

The pre-financing stage involves conducting a risk assessment before actual financing. It involves the following steps:

- ***Identifying the project plan:*** This step ensures a project's alignment with the entities' short-term and long-term goals.

- ***Listing the risks and minimising them:*** This step lists the risks associated with the project and methods to minimise them so it does not affect the project at a later stage.

- ***Checking the feasibility of the project:*** This step involves assessing a project's financial and technical feasibility.

4.11.2.2. Financing stage

The financial stage involves raising capital for project initiation. It involves the following steps:

- ***Listing potential investors:*** This step involves collecting details of potential investors whose goals align with the project's goals and who can benefit from investing in it.

- ***Negotiating the contract:*** This step involves the sponsors and lenders negotiating to finalise an agreement that can benefit both parties.

- ***Documenting the process:*** This step requires documenting the terms and conditions of the agreement and other financial details.

- ***Processing the transactions:*** In this step, the sponsors receive funds to start their operations.

4.11.2.3. Post-financing stage

The post-financial stage involves monitoring the progress of the project at regular intervals. It involves the following steps:

- ***Monitoring the project:*** Project managers require tracking the project at regular intervals to ensure that it does not exceed the assigned budget and follows the set timeline.

- ***Closing the project:*** This step denotes the completion of the project.

- ***Repaying the loans:*** In this step, the sponsors require keeping track of the project's cash flow and ensure that they repay the loans on time.

4.11.3 Benefits of Project Finance

The advantages of project finance include:

- ***It is a type of non-recourse debt.*** Non-recourse debt is favourable for sponsors as they have no obligation to pay additional compensation if they default, except for liquidating their assets.

- ***It maximises leverage.*** As large projects require extensive capital to finance the development and manufacturing costs, sponsors usually fund a major part of the project using debt, which refers to highly leveraged finance. High leverage allows sponsors to finance their projects without diluting their equity with a minimal obligation on repayments.

- ***It provides an off-balance sheet treatment.*** Depending on the project's financial structure, sponsors may not require reporting the debt on its balance sheet, as this is a type of non-recourse debt. This allows them to take further debt to finance other projects.

- ***It enables risk sharing.*** Project financing allows sponsors to share risk with other parties. They do this by paying additional premiums to third-party companies willing to take risks associated with the project.

4.11.4 Limitations of Project Financing

The limitations associated with project financing include:

- ***It is complex.*** Project financing involves negotiations with multiple participants in the project, which can get complicated and expensive. The process is also time-consuming and resource-intensive when compared to direct financing.

- ***It has higher transaction costs.*** Project financing involves higher transactional costs when compared to direct financing because of multiple contracting costs, which are part of the financial structure of a project. This can include legal expenses and extensive documentation related to borrowing, stock issuance and ownership.

- ***It requires constant expert assistance.*** Project financing involves multiple parties and complex transactions. This requires sponsors and other parties to pay additional fees to investment bankers and other professionals to monitor and review the entire process.

- ***It requires ensuring compliance at each step.*** As project financing involves multiple parties, financial institutions require ensuring compliance with laws issued by the government. This requires tracking every transaction, documenting tax filings and filing paperwork to ensure that there is no tax evasion or illegal movement of funds.

4.11.5 Types of Loans for Project Finance

Here are some types of loans that sponsors take to finance the SPV:

4.11.5.1 Pure equity

Equity investors may invest in a project company's operations for partial ownership of the company. The company dilutes its ownership and distributes shares to investors based on the capital they invest. It can start paying dividends to stockholders once it generates cash flow upon completion. If it goes bankrupt, the equity stockholders are the last to receive their payments upon liquidation.

4.11.5.2 Syndicate loans

Two or more lenders collate to provide loans to the project company. In loan syndication, each lender is only responsible for their share of the loan in the total loan amount. In the loan syndication process, one bank assumes the role of an arranging bank on behalf of other banks. This bank is responsible for discussing the terms and conditions of the loan, the repayment period and enforcing contractual obligations.

4.11.5.3 Government loans

Governments provide additional capital for a project to ensure its faster completion for the welfare of the public. They can provide loan funds to the project through direct or indirect financing. Direct financing refers to the funds borrowed directly from the source without a third party's intervention, whereas indirect financing is a means of financing a company through a third-party lender. The advantage of securing government loans is that the borrower may not require paying them back. Governments also provide tax benefits and waiving duties and reduce the political risk associated with economic instability and change of political parties. This encourages institutional investors, foundations and high-net-worth investors to invest in government-supported projects.

Exercise

1. How do you estimate the total cost of a project, and what factors should be considered in this estimation process?

2. What are some common methods used for estimating working capital needs in project financing?

3. What are the different sources of funds available for project financing, and how do they vary in terms of risk and cost?

4. How do project financiers assess the suitability of each funding source for a specific project?

5. Can you discuss the advantages and disadvantages of using debt financing versus equity financing in project finance?

6. What is capital budgeting, and why is it essential in project finance?

7. What are the key methods used for evaluating investment projects in capital budgeting, and how do they differ?

8. How do you identify and assess the various types of risks and uncertainties associated with a project?

9. What strategies can be employed to mitigate and manage risks in project evaluation and decision-making?

10. What are the key components of a projected balance sheet, and how do you prepare one for a project?

11. What is a detailed project report (DPR), and what information does it typically include?

12. How do you structure a DPR to effectively communicate the technical, financial, and operational aspects of a project?

Unit – 5

Social Entrepreneurship

Social Entrepreneurship: Social Sector Perspectives and Social Entrepreneurship, Social Entrepreneurship Opportunities and Successful Models, Social Innovations and Sustainability, Marketing Management for Social Ventures, Risk Management in Social Enterprises, Legal Framework for Social Ventures.

5.1 Social Entrepreneurship

The phrase 'social entrepreneurship' refers to a brand of entrepreneurship rooted in funding or implementing solutions to cultural, social, or environmental problems. The term is something of a catch-all that covers virtually any type of private organization that uses business as a means to socially conscious ends.

Social entrepreneurship is a relatively fluid concept that covers a broad variety of organizations. There's no definitive mold that says, "A socially entrepreneurial business generates X amount of revenue within the confines of a Y organizational structure for a Z type of cause."

For instance, both a mutual aid fund dedicated to assisting small businesses in marginalized communities and a corporation that uses its proceeds to support education for women in third-world countries could both be considered socially entrepreneurial outlets.

Some social enterprises might not follow any sort of typical organizational structure — they can be run entirely by volunteers who do not receive a pay-check or individual contributors that participate of their own accord.

5.1.1 Socialpreneur

A socialpreneur is a person that sets out on an entrepreneurial venture with the intention of addressing social issues and contributing to the social good. These businesses can have a for-profit, non-profit, or hybrid model, but funds are typically used to support operational costs and develop programs to support target markets.

While socialpreneurs still abide by most core tenets as conventional entrepreneurs, there are key differences between the two groups.

5.1.2 Socialpreneur vs. Entrepreneur

Below is a comparison table highlighting the key differences between a Socialpreneur and an Entrepreneur?

Aspect	Socialpreneur	Entrepreneur
Goal	Focus on addressing social or environmental challenges while generating revenue.	Focus primarily on profit-making and financial sustainability.
Business Purpose	Aims to create positive social impact alongside financial sustainability.	Focuses on creating value for customers and stakeholders while maximizing profits.
Revenue Generation	May prioritize social impact over profit generation.	Primary focus on generating profits and financial returns.
Success Metrics	Includes social impact metrics alongside financial performance.	Primarily measured by financial indicators such as revenue, profit margins,

		and ROI.
Funding	May seek funding from impact investors, grants, donations, or social impact investment funds.	Typically seeks funding from venture capital, angel investors, banks, or through bootstrapping.
Market Consideration	Targets underserved or marginalized markets with social needs or environmental concerns.	Targets mainstream or niche markets based on consumer demand and market trends.
Risk Tolerance	May accept lower financial returns or longer time horizons to achieve social impact goals.	Typically focused on maximizing returns and may have higher risk tolerance for innovative ventures.
Brand Identity	Emphasizes social or environmental values and purpose-driven mission.	Often focuses on building a strong brand identity and market presence.
Legal Structure	May choose legal structures such as Benefit Corporation or Social Enterprise.	Can opt for various legal structures such as sole proprietorship, LLC, or corporation.

This table provides a simplified comparison between Socialpreneurs and Entrepreneurs, highlighting their different focuses, goals, and approaches to business.

5.1.3 Examples of Social Entrepreneurship:

Some examples of Social Entrepreneurship are:

- TranSanta
- Books to Prisoners
- Cracked It
- 734 Coffee

- Belu
- Tranquiliti
- Surfrider Foundation
- SOIL
- TOMS
- Ben & Jerry's
- Warby Parker
- Good Eggs
- Lush
- Uncommon Goods
- GoldieBlox
- Pipeline Angels
- United By Blue
- Shea Radiance
- Werk
- Oliberté
- LSTN Sound Co.
- FIGS
- Love Your Melon
- Helpsy
- Cape Clasp
- Better World Books

5.1.1 Key Success Factors of Social Ventures

An exploratory qualitative field study identifies various key factors that influence the success of social entrepreneurial ventures:

- Entrepreneurs' social network
- Total dedication to the venture's success
- Capital base available at the establishment stage
- Acceptance of the venture idea in the public discourse
- Composition of the venturing team, including the ratio of volunteers to salaried employees
- Forming long-term cooperation in the public and non-profit sectors
- Ability of the venture to stand the market test
- Entrepreneurs' previous managerial experience

5.2 Social Sector Perspectives and Social Entrepreneurship

Let's define each term separately:

Social Sector Perspectives

Social sector perspectives refer to the viewpoints, principles, and approaches adopted by organizations and stakeholders operating within the social sector. The social sector, also known as the third sector or non-profit sector, encompasses organizations and initiatives that are primarily focused on addressing social, environmental, and community needs rather than maximizing profits.

Social sector perspectives include:

- ***Mission-driven Focus:*** Organizations in the social sector are guided by a mission to create positive social impact, improve quality of life, and address societal challenges. Their primary goal is to serve the public good rather than generate financial returns for shareholders.

- ***Community Engagement:*** Social sector organizations often prioritize community engagement, participation, and empowerment. They work closely with beneficiaries and stakeholders to co-create solutions, build trust, and ensure that interventions are responsive to local needs and preferences.

- ***Impact Measurement and Evaluation:*** Impact measurement and evaluation are central to social sector perspectives. Organizations seek to assess and demonstrate the effectiveness and outcomes of their programs and interventions, using metrics, data, and qualitative assessments to track progress, inform decision-making, and enhance accountability.

- ***Collaboration and Partnerships:*** Collaboration and partnerships are key principles in the social sector. Organizations often collaborate with governments, businesses, nonprofits, academia, and communities to leverage resources, share expertise, and scale their impact. Partnerships enable organizations to maximize their reach, effectiveness, and sustainability.

- ***Ethical Leadership and Values-Based Management:*** Ethical leadership, integrity, and values-based management are fundamental principles in the social sector. Organizations prioritize transparency, accountability, and social responsibility in their operations, governance, and relationships with stakeholders. They uphold ethical standards and adhere to principles of equity, diversity, and inclusion.

- ***Advocacy and Systems Change:*** Social sector organizations engage in advocacy, policy reform, and systems change efforts to address root causes of social problems, influence public policies, and advocate for marginalized communities. They seek to drive systemic change, challenge structural inequalities, and promote social justice and human rights.

- ***Social Entrepreneurship:*** Social entrepreneurship refers to the practice of using entrepreneurial principles and innovative approaches to create positive social or environmental impact. Social entrepreneurs identify social problems, develop innovative solutions, and mobilize resources to implement and scale their ventures. Key characteristics of social entrepreneurship include:

- ***Social Mission:*** Social entrepreneurship is guided by a clear social or environmental mission. Social entrepreneurs are driven by a desire to address pressing social issues, create positive change, and improve people's lives or the planet.

- ***Innovative Solutions:*** Social entrepreneurs develop innovative solutions to address social problems. They apply creative thinking, entrepreneurial skills, and interdisciplinary approaches to design new products, services, business models, or technologies that tackle social challenges in novel ways.

- ***Financial Sustainability:*** While social entrepreneurs prioritize social impact, they also recognize the importance of financial sustainability. They seek to generate revenue, secure funding, or establish revenue-generating enterprises to support their social missions and sustain their operations over the long term.

- ***Measurement and Accountability:*** Social entrepreneurs measure and evaluate their impact to assess the effectiveness and outcomes of their ventures. They use metrics, data analytics, and qualitative assessments to track progress, demonstrate results, and improve performance. They are accountable to stakeholders, funders, and beneficiaries.

- ***Collaboration and Partnerships:*** Social entrepreneurs collaborate with diverse stakeholders, including governments, nonprofits, businesses, academia, and communities, to achieve their social missions. They forge partnerships, leverage networks, and mobilize resources to maximize their impact, scale their ventures, and address complex social challenges.

- ***Adaptive Leadership:*** Social entrepreneurship requires adaptive leadership skills to navigate uncertainty, overcome challenges, and drive change. Social entrepreneurs demonstrate resilience, flexibility, and perseverance in pursuing their social missions, adapting their strategies to evolving circumstances and seizing opportunities for innovation and growth.

How the perspectives of the social sector contribute to the concept and practice of social entrepreneurship:

- ***Understanding Social Issues:*** Social sector perspectives provide deep insights into the root causes and complexities of social issues such as poverty, inequality, education gaps, environmental degradation, and healthcare disparities. This understanding is essential for social entrepreneurs to identify and prioritize areas where their innovations can have the most significant impact.

- ***Community Engagement:*** Social sector organizations often work closely with communities affected by social problems, fostering trust, collaboration, and grassroots involvement. Social entrepreneurs draw upon these community engagement strategies to co-create solutions that are contextually relevant and sustainable, ensuring they meet the needs and aspirations of the people they serve.

- ***Impact Measurement and Evaluation:*** The social sector places a strong emphasis on impact measurement and evaluation to assess the effectiveness and outcomes of social programs and interventions. Social entrepreneurs adopt similar approaches, using metrics, data analytics, and qualitative assessments to track their social, environmental, and financial performance. This enables them to demonstrate their impact to stakeholders, attract funding, and continuously improve their interventions.

- ***Partnerships and Collaboration:*** Collaboration and partnerships are fundamental principles in the social sector, as organizations often work together to leverage resources, share expertise, and scale their impact. Social entrepreneurs embrace this collaborative mindset, forging partnerships with governments, nonprofits, corporations, academia, and other stakeholders to mobilize resources, access networks, and amplify their reach and influence.

- ***Innovative Financing Models:*** Social sector organizations explore innovative financing models such as impact investing, social impact bonds, crowdfunding, and revenue-generating enterprises to diversify funding sources and sustain their operations. Social entrepreneurs leverage these financing models to attract investment capital, generate revenue, and achieve financial sustainability while pursuing their social missions.

- ***Policy Advocacy and Systems Change:*** The social sector often engages in policy advocacy and systems change efforts to address structural barriers, advocate for marginalized communities, and drive systemic reform. Social entrepreneurs play a crucial role in catalyzing change by challenging the status quo, influencing policy decisions, and pioneering innovative solutions that disrupt entrenched systems and practices.

- ***Ethical Leadership and Values-Based Management:*** Ethical leadership, integrity, and values-based management are core principles in the social sector, guiding organizations' actions and decision-making processes. Social entrepreneurs uphold these principles, demonstrating a commitment to transparency, accountability, and social responsibility in their ventures. They prioritize the triple bottom line—people, planet, and profit—and strive to create shared value for all stakeholders.

- ***Resilience and Adaptability:*** Social sector organizations demonstrate resilience and adaptability in the face of challenges such as funding constraints, political instability, and external shocks. Social entrepreneurs exhibit similar qualities, navigating uncertainty, pivoting their strategies, and innovating new solutions to address emerging needs and opportunities in rapidly changing environments.

5.3 Social Entrepreneurship Opportunities and Successful Models

Let's define each term separately:

- ***Social Entrepreneurship Opportunities:*** Social entrepreneurship opportunities refer to the potential avenues or initiatives where entrepreneurial efforts can be directed to address social or environmental challenges while also generating sustainable solutions and impact. These opportunities arise from identifying pressing social needs or problems and leveraging entrepreneurial principles to develop innovative solutions. Key aspects of social entrepreneurship opportunities include:

- ***Identification of Social Needs:*** Social entrepreneurship opportunities begin with the identification of social or environmental needs, problems, or gaps that impact individuals, communities, or the planet. These needs may include issues such as poverty, education disparities, healthcare access, environmental degradation, or social inequality.

- ***Innovative Solutions:*** Social entrepreneurship opportunities involve the development of innovative solutions to address identified social needs or challenges. Entrepreneurs apply creative thinking, interdisciplinary approaches, and entrepreneurial skills to design new products, services, business models, or technologies that offer sustainable and scalable solutions.

- ***Market Demand:*** Successful social entrepreneurship opportunities are often based on a clear understanding of market demand and user preferences. Entrepreneurs assess the needs and preferences of target beneficiaries, customers, or stakeholders to ensure that their solutions are relevant, accessible, and impactful.

- ***Scalability and Impact:*** Social entrepreneurship opportunities aim to create scalable and impactful solutions that address systemic social or environmental issues. Entrepreneurs seek opportunities to scale their ventures, expand their reach, and maximize their positive impact on individuals, communities, or ecosystems.

- ***Financial Sustainability:*** Social entrepreneurship opportunities emphasize financial sustainability alongside social impact. Entrepreneurs explore revenue-generating models, funding sources, and investment opportunities to ensure the long-term viability and sustainability of their ventures while fulfilling their social missions.

5.3.1 Successful Models of Social Entrepreneurship:

Successful models of social entrepreneurship represent innovative approaches, strategies, or frameworks that have demonstrated effectiveness in creating positive social or environmental impact while achieving financial sustainability. These models showcase various ways in which social entrepreneurs can address social needs, mobilize resources, and drive change. Examples of successful models of social entrepreneurship include:

- ***Hybrid Business Models:*** Hybrid business models integrate social or environmental missions with revenue-generating activities. Examples include Benefit Corporations (B Corps), social enterprises, and social businesses that prioritize both financial sustainability and social impact.

- ***Tech for Good:*** Tech for Good models leverage technology and innovation to address social or environmental challenges. Examples include social enterprises that develop apps, platforms, or digital solutions to improve access to education, healthcare, financial services, or environmental monitoring.

- ***Microfinance and Social Finance:*** Microfinance and social finance models provide financial services, such as microloans, savings accounts, or insurance, to underserved communities or entrepreneurs in developing countries or marginalized populations. Examples include microfinance institutions (MFIs), community development financial institutions (CDFIs), and peer-to-peer lending platforms.

- ***Social Innovation Incubators and Accelerators:*** Social innovation incubators and accelerators support social entrepreneurs by providing mentorship, training, networking, and funding opportunities. Examples include organizations such as Ashoka, Echoing Green, Skoll Foundation, and Unreasonable Group that nurture and scale social entrepreneurship initiatives.

- ***Impact Investing and Social Venture Capital:*** Impact investing and social venture capital models provide funding to social entrepreneurs and enterprises that generate both financial returns and positive social or environmental impact. Examples include impact investors, social impact bonds, and impact-focused venture capital funds that prioritize double or triple bottom-line outcomes.

- ***Community-Based Enterprises:*** Community-based enterprises empower local communities to address their own social and economic needs through cooperative ownership, participatory decision-making, and shared ownership structures. Examples include community-owned renewable energy projects, worker cooperatives, and community land trusts.

5.4 Social Innovations and Sustainability

Social innovations and sustainability are closely interconnected concepts that aim to address pressing social and environmental challenges while promoting long-term well-being and resilience. Here's an overview of how social innovations contribute to sustainability:

5.4.1 Definition of Social Innovations

Social innovations involve the development and implementation of novel solutions to address social, environmental, or economic issues. These innovations can take various forms, including new products, services, business models, policies, technologies, or practices. Social innovations are driven by a desire to create positive change, improve quality of life, and foster inclusive and sustainable development.

5.4.2 Link between Social Innovations and Sustainability

Social innovations play a crucial role in advancing sustainability goals by addressing systemic challenges and promoting equitable and environmentally responsible practices. They contribute to sustainability in the following ways:

Addressing Social and Environmental Issues: Social innovations target a wide range of social and environmental issues, including poverty, inequality, climate change, and resource depletion, pollution, and biodiversity loss. By developing innovative solutions to these challenges, social innovators contribute to the achievement of sustainability objectives.

Promoting Inclusive Development: Social innovations often focus on promoting inclusive development by empowering marginalized communities, enhancing access to essential services (such as healthcare, education, and clean energy), and reducing social disparities. Inclusive development is a core component of sustainability, as it ensures that progress benefits all members of society, including vulnerable and marginalized groups.

Encouraging Collaboration and Partnerships: Social innovations foster collaboration and partnerships among diverse stakeholders, including governments, businesses, nonprofits, academia, and communities. These partnerships facilitate the co-creation and implementation of innovative solutions, leveraging the collective expertise, resources, and networks of multiple actors to address complex social and environmental challenges.

Driving Systemic Change: Social innovations have the potential to drive systemic change by challenging existing norms, structures, and practices that contribute to social and environmental problems. They introduce disruptive ideas, models, and approaches that inspire new ways of thinking and acting, leading to transformative shifts in attitudes, behaviors, policies, and institutions.

Promoting Resilience and Adaptation: Social innovations contribute to building resilience and adaptation to environmental and socio-economic shocks and stresses. They empower communities to cope with and recover from disasters, climate change impacts, economic downturns, and other crises by fostering adaptive capacity, social cohesion, and local empowerment.

Encouraging Responsible Consumption and Production: Social innovations promote responsible consumption and production patterns by encouraging sustainable lifestyles, circular economy practices, waste reduction, recycling, and resource efficiency. They advocate for alternative models of production and consumption that prioritize environmental conservation, social equity, and economic prosperity.

Fostering Innovation Ecosystems: Social innovations contribute to the development of vibrant innovation ecosystems that support creativity, entrepreneurship, and collaboration. They create opportunities for experimentation, learning, and knowledge sharing, fostering a culture of innovation and continuous improvement that drives sustainable development.

5.4.3 Examples of Social Innovations for Sustainability

Sustainable agriculture practices that promote regenerative farming, organic agriculture, agroforestry, and permaculture.

Renewable energy technologies and clean energy solutions such as solar power, wind energy, and hydroelectricity.

Circular economy initiatives that reduce waste, promote resource efficiency, and encourage product reuse, recycling, and remanufacturing.

Social enterprises that provide affordable and accessible healthcare, education, sanitation, and clean water solutions to underserved communities.

Urban innovations such as green buildings, sustainable transportation systems, urban agriculture, and smart city technologies that enhance livability and reduce environmental impacts.

Community-based conservation and natural resource management initiatives that empower local communities to protect and steward biodiversity, forests, oceans, and other ecosystems.

5.5 Marketing Management for Social Ventures

Marketing management for social ventures involves applying marketing principles and strategies to promote social causes, drive positive change, and achieve sustainable impact. While the ultimate goal of social ventures is to create social value rather than solely maximizing profits, effective marketing remains essential for raising awareness, mobilizing support, and maximizing the reach and impact of their initiatives. Here's how marketing management can be tailored to the unique needs and objectives of social ventures:

5.5.1 Understanding Stakeholders and Target Audience:

Social ventures must identify and understand their stakeholders, including beneficiaries, donors, partners, volunteers, policymakers, and the broader community. Conducting stakeholder analysis helps to identify their needs, preferences, motivations, and communication preferences.

Segmenting the target audience based on demographic, psychographic, and behavioral factors allows social ventures to tailor their marketing messages, channels, and approaches to different audience segments effectively.

5.5.2 Crafting Compelling Messaging and Storytelling:

Effective storytelling is crucial for engaging stakeholders and inspiring action. Social ventures should articulate a clear and compelling narrative that communicates their mission, impact, values, and the importance of supporting their cause.

Messaging should resonate with the emotions and values of the target audience, highlighting the human stories behind the social issue and demonstrating the tangible benefits of supporting the venture's initiatives.

5.5.3 Building Brand Identity and Trust:

Establishing a strong brand identity builds credibility, trust, and recognition for the social venture. Branding should reflect the organization's values, mission, and unique value proposition, distinguishing it from competitors and reinforcing its authenticity and integrity.

Consistent branding across all communication channels, including website, social media, print materials, and events, helps to reinforce brand recognition and trust among stakeholders.

5.5.4 Utilizing Digital and Social Media Marketing:

Digital and social media platforms offer powerful tools for reaching and engaging target audiences cost-effectively. Social ventures should leverage these channels to share compelling content, engage with followers, and mobilize support for their cause.

Content marketing strategies, such as blogs, videos, infographics, and user-generated content, can help to educate, inspire, and activate supporters, driving traffic to the organization's website and social media profiles.

5.5.5 Engaging Influencers and Advocates:

Collaborating with influencers, thought leaders, and advocates can amplify the reach and impact of social ventures' marketing efforts. Influencers with aligned values and interests can help to raise awareness, drive donations, and mobilize support through their networks and platforms.

Building relationships with grassroots advocates, volunteers, and community leaders can also enhance outreach and engagement at the local level, fostering a sense of ownership and belonging among stakeholders.

5.5.6 Measuring and Evaluating Impact:

Social ventures should establish key performance indicators (KPIs) to measure the effectiveness of their marketing efforts and track progress towards their goals. Metrics may include website traffic, social media engagement, email open rates, donation conversion rates, and brand sentiment.

Regular monitoring and evaluation allow social ventures to assess the ROI of their marketing activities, identify areas for improvement, and make data-driven decisions to optimize their marketing strategy over time.

5.5.7 Fostering Collaboration and Partnerships:

Collaborating with other organizations, businesses, and community groups can extend the reach and impact of social ventures' marketing initiatives. Partnerships can involve joint campaigns, co-branded events, cross-promotions, or shared resources to amplify messaging and leverage complementary strengths.

Strategic partnerships with media outlets, corporate sponsors, influencers, and advocacy groups can provide access to new audiences, resources, and expertise, enhancing the effectiveness and sustainability of marketing efforts.

By integrating these marketing management principles and strategies into their operations, social ventures can effectively raise awareness, mobilize support, and drive meaningful change in their communities and beyond. Effective marketing not only enhances the visibility and impact of social ventures but also strengthens their sustainability and ability to achieve their social missions over the long term.

5.6 Risk Management in Social Enterprises

Risk management in social enterprises involves identifying, assessing, mitigating, and monitoring risks that could impact the organization's ability to achieve its social mission and financial sustainability. While social enterprises operate with the primary goal of creating positive social impact, they are still subject to various risks inherent in any business endeavor. Here's how social enterprises can effectively manage risks:

5.6.1 Identifying Risks

Social enterprises should conduct a comprehensive risk assessment to identify potential threats and vulnerabilities that could affect their operations, stakeholders, and ability to achieve their social goals.

Risks may include financial risks (such as funding shortages or cash flow problems), operational risks (such as supply chain disruptions or regulatory compliance issues), reputational risks (such as negative publicity or stakeholder dissatisfaction), and strategic risks (such as changes in market conditions or competitive threats).

5.6.2 Assessing Risks:

Once risks are identified, social enterprises should assess the likelihood and potential impact of each risk on their organization. This involves analyzing the probability of occurrence, severity of consequences, and speed of onset for different risk scenarios.

Risk assessment helps prioritize risks based on their significance and urgency, allowing social enterprises to allocate resources effectively to address the most critical threats.

5.6.3 Mitigating Risks

After assessing risks, social enterprises should develop risk mitigation strategies to reduce the likelihood and impact of identified risks. Mitigation strategies may include implementing internal controls, diversifying funding sources, establishing contingency plans, and enhancing resilience through capacity building and adaptive management practices.

Social enterprises should also consider transferring or sharing risks through insurance, partnerships, or contractual arrangements to minimize their exposure to certain risks beyond their control.

5.6.4 Monitoring Risks

Risk management is an ongoing process that requires continuous monitoring and review. Social enterprises should establish mechanisms for monitoring key risk indicators, tracking changes in the risk landscape, and assessing the effectiveness of risk mitigation measures.

Regular risk assessments and reviews allow social enterprises to adapt their strategies and responses to evolving threats, emerging opportunities, and changing external conditions.

5.6.5 Embedding Risk Management in Governance and Culture

Effective risk management requires strong leadership, governance, and a culture of risk awareness and accountability throughout the organization. Social enterprises should integrate risk management into their decision-making processes, strategic planning, and day-to-day operations.

Boards of directors and senior management should provide oversight and guidance on risk management practices, ensuring that risks are considered systematically and addressed proactively to safeguard the organization's mission and values.

5.6.6 Engaging Stakeholders

Social enterprises should engage stakeholders, including employees, beneficiaries, donors, partners, and communities, in risk management efforts. Stakeholder involvement can provide valuable insights, perspectives, and resources for identifying, assessing, and mitigating risks effectively.

Transparent communication and stakeholder engagement foster trust, collaboration, and shared responsibility for managing risks, enhancing the organization's resilience and sustainability over the long term.

5.6.7 Learning from Failures and Successes

Social enterprises should embrace a culture of learning and continuous improvement, recognizing that failures and setbacks are inherent to innovation and growth. By analyzing past failures and successes, social enterprises can identify lessons learned, best practices, and areas for improvement in their risk management processes.

Learning from failures helps social enterprises build resilience, adaptability, and agility in navigating uncertainty and complexity, ultimately strengthening their ability to achieve their social mission and create lasting impact.

5.7 Legal Framework for Social Ventures

The legal framework for social ventures encompasses a range of legal structures and regulations that govern the formation, operation, and governance of organizations dedicated to pursuing social or environmental missions while generating financial returns. Choosing the right legal structure is crucial for social ventures, as it determines factors such as liability, tax treatment, governance requirements, and access to funding. Here are some common legal structures and considerations for social ventures:

5.7.1 For-Profit Legal Structures

- ***Benefit Corporation (B Corp):*** B Corps are for-profit corporations that are legally required to consider the impact of their decisions on stakeholders, including workers, communities, and the environment, in addition to shareholders. B Corps must meet rigorous social and environmental performance standards and report annually on their impact.

- **Social Purpose Corporation (SPC):** Similar to B Corps, SPCs are for-profit corporations that prioritize social or environmental goals alongside financial objectives. SPCs have flexibility in defining their social purpose and are subject to specific reporting requirements on their social and environmental performance.

5.7.2 Hybrid Legal Structures

- **Flexible Purpose Corporation (FPC):** FPCs are hybrid entities that blend elements of for-profit and nonprofit legal structures. FPCs have a primary purpose of achieving social or environmental goals but can also generate profits for shareholders. They have greater flexibility in pursuing their social mission than traditional for-profit entities.

- **Community Interest Company (CIC):** CICs are hybrid entities commonly used in the United Kingdom and other countries. CICs are for-profit companies with a social mission, and they must demonstrate their commitment to community benefit through a "community interest statement" and asset lock provisions.

5.7.3 Nonprofit Legal Structures:

- **Nonprofit Corporation:** Nonprofit corporations are tax-exempt entities that operate exclusively for charitable, educational, religious, or other exempt purposes. Nonprofits can pursue social or environmental missions and are eligible for tax-deductible donations and grants but are subject to restrictions on profit distribution and activities.

- **501(c)(3) Organization:** In the United States, organizations seeking federal tax-exempt status under Section 501(c)(3) of the Internal Revenue Code must meet specific requirements, including operating exclusively for charitable, educational, or other exempt purposes, and engaging in limited political activities.

- ***Charitable Trust or Foundation:*** Charitable trusts or foundations are legal entities established to hold and manage assets for charitable purposes. They distribute funds to nonprofit organizations or directly undertake charitable activities, such as grantmaking, scholarship programs, or social initiatives.

5.7.4 Cooperative Legal Structures

- ***Worker Cooperative:*** Worker cooperatives are businesses owned and democratically controlled by their employees. They operate based on cooperative principles, including voluntary and open membership, democratic control, and equitable distribution of profits.

- ***Community-Owned Cooperative:*** Community-owned cooperatives are owned and governed by community members and may operate in various sectors, including housing, agriculture, energy, and consumer goods. They prioritize community benefit and participation in decision-making.

5.7.5 Legal Considerations for Social Ventures

- ***Mission Alignment:*** Choose a legal structure that aligns with the organization's mission, values, and long-term goals. Consider whether the legal structure provides sufficient flexibility and accountability to pursue social or environmental objectives effectively.

- ***Liability Protection:*** Evaluate the level of liability protection offered by different legal structures. For-profit entities typically provide limited liability protection for owners, while nonprofit entities may offer broader immunity from liability.

- ***Tax Implications:*** Understand the tax implications associated with each legal structure, including corporate taxes, income taxes, and eligibility for tax-exempt status. Consider the impact on fundraising, donations, grants, and earned income streams.

- ***Governance Requirements:*** Consider the governance requirements, reporting obligations, and fiduciary duties associated with each legal structure. Ensure that the governance structure aligns with the organization's values and promotes transparency, accountability, and stakeholder participation.

- ***Access to Capital:*** Assess the organization's ability to raise capital, attract investors, and access financing under different legal structures. Consider the preferences of impact investors, philanthropic funders, and other stakeholders in the social finance ecosystem.

Exercise

1. What are the key principles and values that guide social sector organizations, and how do they intersect with the objectives of social entrepreneurship?

2. How do social entrepreneurs navigate the complexities of balancing social impact with financial sustainability, and what strategies do they employ to achieve both goals?

3. What are some successful models of social entrepreneurship that have demonstrated effectiveness in creating positive social impact while achieving financial sustainability?

4. How do social entrepreneurship initiatives measure and evaluate their impact, and what lessons can be learned from successful models to inform future strategies and approaches?

5. How do social innovations contribute to advancing sustainability goals and addressing environmental, social, and economic challenges?

6. What are some examples of social innovations that promote sustainable development, environmental conservation, and resilience in communities and ecosystems?

7. How can social innovation ecosystems support the creation and scaling of innovative solutions to complex social and environmental problems?

8. What role do partnerships between social entrepreneurs, governments, businesses, and civil society organizations play in fostering innovation for sustainability?

9. How do social innovations promote responsible consumption and production patterns, circular economy practices, and inclusive growth models that benefit people and the planet?

10. How can social ventures effectively communicate their social mission, values, and impact to stakeholders through marketing and branding strategies?

11. How do social ventures differentiate themselves in the marketplace and build brand loyalty and trust among consumers, donors, and partners?

12. What role do storytelling, content marketing, and advocacy campaigns play in shaping public perceptions, influencing behavior change, and driving social impact for social ventures?

13. How can social ventures measure the effectiveness and ROI of their marketing efforts and adapt their strategies to optimize impact and engagement over time?

14. What role does governance, leadership, and organizational culture play in promoting risk awareness, resilience, and adaptability in social enterprises?

*** END ***

9 798889 291524